CH00602008

Miracles

Philosophy of Religion Study Guide

Clare Jarmy

First published 2013

by PushMe Press

Mid Somerset House, Southover, Wells, Somerset BA5 1UH

www.pushmepress.com

© 2014 Inducit Learning Ltd

The right of Clare Jarmy to be identified as author of this work has been asserted by her in accordance with sections 77 and 78 of the Copyright, Designs and Patents Act 1988.

All rights reserved. No part of this book may be reprinted or reproduced or utilised in any form or transmitted by any electronic, mechanical, or other means, now known or hereafter invented, including photocopying and recording, or in any information storage or retrieval system, without permission in writing from the publishers.

British Library Cataloguing in Publication Data
A catalogue record for this book is available from the British Library

ISBN: 978-1-909618-48-0 (pbk)
ISBN: 978-1-910252-98-7 (hbk)
ISBN: 978-1-909618-49-7 (ebk)
ISBN: 978-1-910252-99-4 (pdf)

Typeset in Frutiger by booksellerate.com
Printed by Lightning Source

A rich & engaging community assisted by the best teachers in Philosophy

philosophy.pushmepress.com

Students and teachers explore Philosophy of Religion through handouts, film clips, presentations, case studies, extracts, games and academic articles.

Pitched just right, and so much more than a textbook, here is a place to engage with critical reflection whatever your level. Marked student essays are also posted.

Contents

Please support our learning community by not photocopying without a licence

Definitions

Any discussion of miracles, and whether they could ever happen, must first begin with a discussion of the **DIFFERENT DEFINITIONS** that could be given of a miracle. In order to discuss a subject, you have to understand what the subject is. If you do not know how to define justice, how do you know what a just person is? If you do not know what is meant by knowledge, how do you know if you have it? It is just the same for miracles. If we do not know what we mean by the miraculous, then how can we know whether it is reasonable to think miracles happen?

Preceding a discussion of a topic by formulating a definition is not new. A large number of Socratic dialogues start this way. Typically, Socrates begins by asking a question such as "What is justice?"; "What is love?"; "What is knowledge?". Socrates' interlocutors (the others in the discussion) then offer different definitions, which are examined to see which captures best the subject of discussion. Socrates was right that **HAVING THE RIGHT DEFINITION IS IMPORTANT** before any philosophical discussion can be effective; it is the only way of ensuring that you have a clear idea of the subject, and that people are not talking at cross purposes.

MIRACLE

The word "miracle" comes from the Latin **MIRACULUM**, meaning "wondrous". It is a word we hear often when talking to people, or in news stories. Someone might say that it was a miracle that they made it to the train on time, or that it was a miracle that Andy Murray won Wimbledon on such a hot day. In this sense, the term "miracle" is being used to describe an unlikely event; a lucky event; a good, but unexpected event.

Take this example from the Liverpool Echo from June 2013: "Burt the miracle mog has leg saved with incredible cat bone transplant". This "miracle mog" is undoubtedly very lucky to receive cutting-edge veterinary medicine, but here using the word "miracle" seems to be pushing the notion somewhat.

We know that in these cases, the term "miracle" is being used in a colloquial way. Catching the train, however impressive, should not really be described as miraculous. So if these events do not count as miracles, what sorts of events do? When asked to name a miracle, someone might say "the feeding of the five thousand", or "Jesus turning water into wine at the wedding in Cana". How are these events different from making it to the train, winning Wimbledon on a hot day, or giving a cat the very best treatment?

The definition of miracle that we settle on will determine everything else that we say about miracles, including whether we think they have happened, or could happen. Some definitions of miracles are so tight and precise that they effectively define miracles out of existence; the definition means miracles could never happen. Conversely, some definitions are so liberal that it seems that practically anything could count as a miracle.

So let us now begin to look at some of the most important definitions of miracles.

DAVID HUME

You may well know a little about David Hume already. Hume was a very important figure in the Scottish Enlightenment, which was a time in the 18th C when Scotland, and particularly Edinburgh, could boast a number of important thinkers in various fields. Apart from Hume, the most notable of these was arguably the celebrated economist Adam Smith, who was a friend of Hume and published Hume's controversial Dialogues Concerning Natural Religion after his death.

Hume is now best known as a philosopher: an empiricist, and a sceptic about religion. Hume would perhaps be surprised at this, because much of his work was not actually in the area of 'Philosophy, but in History. In his day he would have been thought of perhaps more as a man of letters; a kind of freelance scholar. But it is now for his work in Philosophy that he is rightly remembered.

If you know anything of Hume's arguments in Dialogues Concerning Natural Religion, you might find it surprising that he formulated a definition of miracles. In this book, Hume effectively destroys much of the Argument from Design, as well as critiquing the Cosmological Argument. Surely someone with this world view would not believe that miracles happen?

Here we see the importance of definition coming into play. As we shall examine later on, Hume believed that miracles do not happen. He gives his definition of miracles, not to explain phenomena he thinks take place, but rather to show precisely what he is rejecting.

In An Enquiry Concerning Human Understanding, Hume defined a miracle as **A TRANSGRESSION OF A LAW OF NATURE BY THE PARTICULAR VOLITION OF THE DEITY OR THE INTERPOSITION**

OF SOME INVISIBLE AGENT. (An Enquiry Concerning Human Understanding, Section X)

According to Hume, a miracle must:

1. Break a law of nature, and either

2. Be caused by the will of God or

3. Be caused by an "invisible agent", which presumably means the actions of angels.

An example of a biblical miracle that would be in accordance with Hume's definition would be the feeding of the five thousand. From five small loaves, and two fishes, Jesus is able to feed five thousand people. In fact, some biblical scholars think it may have been many more than five thousand people, as it is possible that the Gospels refer to five thousand men, not counting women and children. The people who are gathered around Jesus are not only fed; there are twelve baskets of food left over after the feast. The number of calories in five small loaves and two fishes is simply not enough to feed that number of people, and THE **PRINCIPLE OF THE CONSERVATION OF MATTER** means that more bread cannot appear out of nowhere. This miracle clearly meets Hume's criteria. It is "a transgression of the law of nature by the particular volition of the deity".

On the other hand, an example of a biblical miracle that would not meet Hume's criteria is Jesus healing a man with leprosy. Although leprosy is a terrible disease, it is not inconceivable that someone should never be cured of it. It is also not impossible that it should in no case clear up on its own. Jesus' healing action therefore requires no breaking of a law of nature. Hume would therefore not categorise this as a miracle.

We will talk later about what we mean by laws of nature, and whether they could ever be broken, but we can already see that this definition is extremely tight. For Hume, an event that is extraordinary or profoundly unusual is not sufficient; something can only be a miracle if it is an event that runs contrary to nature. We will see later when we examine Hume's critique that his strict definition aids him in undermining the very possibility of a miracle ever taking place.

AQUINAS

Saint Thomas Aquinas, who wrote extensively on the Philosophy of Religion, formulated an understanding of miracles that includes the breaking of a law of nature, but is not limited to it. In the 13th C, when Aquinas was writing, the term "law of nature" was not used to describe the regularity governing the universe. It was more typical to talk about things or events that were in accordance with nature or against nature. Strictly, therefore, Aquinas does not say miracles can break laws of nature, but he does say that miracles can do things which nature cannot, which really amounts to the same thing.

Aquinas listed three types of event that, he thought, should count as miracles:

1. **EVENTS WHICH NATURE COULD NOT PERFORM** - An example of this could be in **JOSHUA 10**, when the sun stops still in the sky, or in **EXODUS 14**, where the Red Sea is parted to allow the people of Israel to escape from Egypt.

2. **EVENTS WHICH NATURE COULD PERFORM, BUT NOT IN THAT ORDER** - An example of this could be when Jesus healed the man born blind. It is possible in nature for someone to become blind. It is not normally possible for a blind man to become sighted; it is certainly not a natural occurrence.

3. **EVENTS WHICH NATURE COULD PERFORM, BUT GOD PERFORMS INSTEAD** - An example of this could be when Jesus calms the storm in **MARK 4**. Eventually the storm would have stopped, but for Jesus to stand in a boat and get the thunder and lightning to cease is an extraordinary event. As the

disciples say: "Who is this? Even the wind and waves obey him!"

The events that count as miracles according to Aquinas are extraordinary by any measure. At the same time, Aquinas allows many more events to be counted as miraculous than Hume does. We must consider here that Aquinas and Hume are coming at the problem from a completely different angle. Hume's definition comes in the context of a critique; Aquinas's definition comes in the context of apologetics, namely writing from a Christian standpoint.

Like Aquinas, CS Lewis is more liberal than Hume on the question of laws of nature, saying that a miracle is "an interference with nature by a supernatural power". His emphasis is therefore very similar to Aquinas', and allows for similar events to be called miraculous. CS Lewis's discussion of God's interference in nature comes within a context of a discussion about the natural and supernatural to which we will allude later.

RICHARD SWINBURNE

Up until now, the definitions that we have looked at have been concerned with exactly what kind of event has happened. Has a law of nature been broken? Could this have happened in the normal run of things? Is this an interference with the natural order? One criticism that could be made about Hume, Aquinas and CS Lewis's definitions is that they focus too much on the event itself, and too little on what it means.

To a religious believer, the extraordinary nature of an event is on its own not enough to call it miraculous. For a start, there is nothing in any of the definitions we have already examined that means the miracle must be a good thing. **RICHARD SWINBURNE** realised that if God caused a toy box to levitate and turn over, spilling all toys on the floor, because nature could not have allowed that to happen, on some accounts this would have to be counted as a miracle. Aquinas or Lewis could contest that the omnibenevolent God of Christianity would never do this, but the point that Swinburne is making here is that their definitions of miracles do not prescribe that the event must be good.

Moreover, the miracle might have significance that goes far beyond its extraordinary nature. It might, for example, be **CHRISTOLOGICAL**; it might tell us about the nature of Jesus. The question of whether an event does or does not break the law of nature is not the only consideration. Swinburne gave an example to explain this. Imagine God altered the laws of nature to enable a feather to fall in a slightly different place than it would have done, had it been left to nature. This would be a breaking of a law of nature, brought about by God. In other words, it would meet Hume's criteria for a miracle. However, this event would be entirely meaningless. This shows that there is more to the miraculous than whether it contravenes laws of nature; miracles should not be meaningless.

8

Swinburne's definition of a miracle is, therefore, **AN EVENT OF AN EXTRAORDINARY KIND, BROUGHT ABOUT BY A GOD, AND OF RELIGIOUS SIGNIFICANCE**. The importance of religious significance shall become apparent when we look later in much greater detail at its place in miracle narratives.

PAUL TILLICH

... an event which is astonishing, unusual, shaking, without contradicting the rational structure of reality. In the second place, it is an event which points to the mystery of being, expressing its relation to us in a definite way. In the third place, it is an occurrence which is received as a sign-event in an ecstatic experience. - Paul Tillich, Systematic Theology, p.117

Another scholar who highlighted the importance of religious significance was Paul Tillich. As you may know if you have studied religious language, Tillich thought that the symbolic aspect of religious language was the most important. He carried this viewpoint through to his work on miracles, where he claimed that miracles were "sign-events". By this, he means that miracles are not meant to be taken as mere historical statements. Rather, it is their significance that is noteworthy. They are events which point to something; something important.

Tillich justifies his view that miracles are sign-events with an appeal to biblical evidence. He points out that Jesus regularly refuses to perform miracles. He does this when the crowd simply wants a demonstration of his power. An example of this is Matthew 13:58, where it says that "he did not do many miracles there **BECAUSE OF THEIR LACK OF FAITH**". Jesus does not perform miracles because he is powerful; he performs miracles "so that you may believe ... and in believing have eternal life in his name". (John 20:30-31)

According to Tillich, the idea of the breaking of a law of nature should not come into the idea of a miracle. Firstly, there is no need for a miracle to break a law of nature, if it is to be seen as a sign-event, where the importance is symbolic and not historical. Secondly, Tillich sees it as intrinsically difficult for the rational basis of the universe to be turned on its head. This would be required, were a law of nature to break. So, unlike Aquinas or Hume, Tillich specifically says that a miracle must be extraordinary, but must not break a law of nature.

It should not be underestimated, however, how important the extraordinary nature of miraculous events is to Tillich. The fact that he does not believe laws of nature should be broken does not nullify the earth-shattering experience of a miracle. He describes miracles as "ecstatic", which literally means "standing outside of oneself". Miraculous experiences transcend all normal experience, and according to Tillich bring you into the presence of God.

RF HOLLAND

A scholar who takes the discussion of religious significance to its logical conclusion is RF Holland. In fact, he goes further than Richard Swinburne and Tillich, making religious significance the only important factor. For Holland, religious significance is an entirely subjective thing; something is significant if it is seen to be significant by the person experiencing the event. RF Holland does not require that an event breaks a law of nature; indeed to him, a miracle could be sheer coincidence. Holland famously used an example of a little boy playing on a railway track:

> *A child riding his toy motor car strays onto an unguarded railway crossing near his house and a wheel of his car gets stuck down the side of one of the rails. An express train is due to pass with the signals in its favour and a curve in the track makes it impossible for the driver to stop his train in time to avoid any obstruction he might encounter on the crossing. The mother coming out of the house to look for her child sees him on the crossing and hears the train approaching. She runs forward shouting and waving. The little boy remains seated in his car, looking downward, engrossed in the task of pedalling it free. The brakes of the train are applied and it comes to a rest a few feet from the child. The mother thanks God for the miracle; which she never ceases to think of as such, although, as she in due course learns, there was nothing supernatural about the manner in which the brakes to the train came to be applied. The driver had fainted, for a reason which had nothing to do with the presence of the child on the line, and the brakes were applied automatically as his hand ceased to exert pressure on the control lever. - RF Holland, The Miraculous, p. 451*

In this example, the mother sees religious significance in the event, irrespective of the fact that it was not brought about by any divine intervention. Holland's view is, therefore, at the opposite end of the spectrum to that of David Hume. Whereas Hume emphasises the idea of a breaking of a law of nature, and its cause being divine, Holland thinks that neither of these is important. As we said at the beginning of this chapter, the former definition makes miracles practically impossible; the latter definition requires very little of an event for it to be deemed miraculous. If, as Holland claims, a miracle can be a **LUCKY COINCIDENCE** that someone interprets as miraculous, then a great many events would surely count. More than this though, the fact that this event seems miraculous to the mother ignores the reaction of the poor train driver's wife when she hears that he fainted at work. This particular "miracle" is contingent upon something unfortunate happening to somebody else.

THE SPECTRUM OF DEFINITIONS

We have examined definitions that give a whole spectrum of different understandings of what a miracle is. Below is a summary of the different views.

PHILOSOPHER	DEFINITION	ATTRIBUTES
David Hume	A transgression of the law of nature by the particular volition of the deity or the interposition of some invisible agent.	1 & 3
Thomas Aquinas	Events which nature could not perform. Events which nature could perform, but not in that order. Events which nature could perform, but not that quickly.	1, 2 & 3
Richard Swinburne	An event of an extraordinary kind, brought about by a god, and of religious significance.	1, 2, 3 & 4
Paul Tillich	An event which is astonishing, unusual, shaking, without contradicting the rational structure of reality; which points to the mystery of being; an occurrence which is received as a sign-event in an ecstatic experience.	2, 3 & 4
RF Holland	An event that could be coincidental, in which someone sees deep religious significance.	4

1 = Miracle breaks a law of nature

2 = Miracle is an extraordinary event, not necessarily breaking a law of nature?

3 = Miracle is brought about by God?

4 = The importance of religious significance is emphasised?

CONCLUSION

The definition used to describe a miracle is vital for all further discussion of the miraculous. If you are working with a tight definition, such as Hume's, the discussion you have will be focused on the question of whether a law of nature can be broken. If, on the other hand, you subscribe to RF Holland's view, it seems clear that miracles do happen, and no discussion of laws of nature is necessary. What we mean by the term "miracle" is contentious, and it is therefore important to be clear about what definition you subscribe to.

KEY TERMS

- **MIRACULUM** - Latin, meaning "wondrous"; the word from which we get our word "miracle".

- **TRANGRESSION** - A breaking of a law or limit of some kind; in this case, we are talking of a law of nature, but we could mean a law of the land, a religious law or even just social convention.

- **VOLITION** - An archaic word meaning "want" or "will". Comes from the same root as "omnibenevolence", which literally means "all good wanting".

- **RELIGIOUS SIGNIFICANCE** - The importance of an event beyond its purely surprising or extraordinary nature. The significance of a miraculous event might be that it shows who Jesus is, or that it relates to key themes in that religious tradition.

- **CHRISTOLOGY** (Christological) - The study of the nature of Jesus. If a miracle has a Christological element to it, it tells us something about Jesus.

- **SIGN-EVENT** - Tillich's term for the symbolic status of miracle narratives. Stories of miracles, to him, are important because of what they reveal, symbolically, about the nature of God.

- **ECSTATIC** - Literally, standing outside yourself. An ecstatic experience is one above and beyond a normal way of existing. This is the third aspect of miraculous occurrences that Tillich focuses on.

SELF-ASSESSMENT QUESTIONS

1. Do miracles have to break laws of nature? What are the benefits of a definition that requires this? What are the drawbacks?

2. What is more important in a definition of miracles: an emphasis on the nature of the event, or on its religious significance?

3. Could one person's miracle entail someone else's tragedy?

FURTHER READING

- **CLACK, B & CLACK, BR** - The Philosophy of Religion: A Critical Introduction, 2nd ed. Polity Press, 2008, pp. 142-144; pp. 148-150

- **COLE, P** - Philosophy of Religion, 2nd ed. Hodder Murray, 2009, pp. 60-64

- **DAVIES, B** - An Introduction to the Philosophy of Religion, 3rd ed. Oxford University Press, 2004, pp. 237-241

- **VARDY, P** - The Puzzle of God, 2nd ed. Fount, 1999, Ch. 17

Nature, the Supernatural & Laws of Nature

Much discussion on the topic of miracles hinges on the question of whether laws of nature can be broken. In this chapter, we will look at what we mean by nature, what we might mean by something supernatural, ie outside of nature, and how we should understand laws of nature.

NATURE

In **CS LEWIS'S BOOK MIRACLES**, Lewis highlights what we might mean by nature by giving a list of different senses in which we use the term. Let us use our own list to examine what "nature" means.

Consider:

- Making a dog eat only vegetarian food is against its nature.

- I was not surprised that the shopkeeper was kind to me; he is very good-natured.

- I used to think she dyed her hair, but actually it's natural.

- The reason I'm so scared of flying is because humans are not meant to fly; it goes against nature.

- In primary schools, children will often make a nature table, where they display things they found outside such as pinecones, snail shells, leaves and seeds.

- I find cocktail parties so artificial. They are not a natural way of socialising; everyone standing there with a drink in one hand and a crisp in the other, trying to make conversation.

What do these statements tell us about nature? Statements 1 and 2 suggest that nature is something intrinsic to a creature. For the dog, it is in his nature to eat meat; for the shopkeeper, it is in his nature to be kind. So, the term "nature" is used to mean something intrinsic; perhaps something that something/someone is born with.

Statements 3 and 6 are using the word "nature" in opposition to something artificial. Dyed hair and cocktail parties are perceived as being artificial (in different ways). Dyed hair is not natural because it requires active interference with your normal hair colour. Cocktail parties are artificial because they prescribe behaviour different from a more comfortable way of socialising. So, in these statements, nature is the normal state of things. Without dye, hair would naturally be a different colour; without the social expectations at cocktail parties, behaviour would be different.

Statement 4 is making a similar point to statements 3 and 6; that flying is not what humans would do if something (the plane) were not interfering in the natural order of things. But statement 4 is going further. Take the phrase "not meant to fly"; if you have studied **ETHICAL NATURALISM**, or **NATURAL MORAL LAW**, you wil recognise this. Statement 4 is not simply saying that nature is something inartificial, but suggests that nature is the way things ought to be. It is not just describing how things are; it is prescribing how things should be.

Statement 5 uses nature to mean "things from the environment around us". It is similar to statements 1, 2, 3 and 6, because the things that make it to the nature-table are not man-made; they can be found lying around in the world. We did not put them there, and picking them up is our first real intervention in their existence.

So, these statements have shown us some important things about our understanding of nature:

- It is what is intrinsic - the nature of a dog is what it intrinsically is; the nature of a person is how they intrinsically are.

- It is what something is when it is not artificial. When something is artificial, its natural state has been disrupted.

- Some people use an idea of what's natural to make prescriptions about what should happen. They might cite the fact that something is unnatural as a reason not to do it.

- Nature is something mankind has no involvement with; it is something we did not design or make. A pinecone is natural; a cathedral is not.

CS Lewis - Naturalism and the Supernatural

CS Lewis claims that there are many who use the term "nature" to mean "everything that exists". Lewis calls these people "naturalists". **NATURALISTS**, Lewis argues, have **A WORLD VIEW THAT MAKES MIRACLES IMPOSSIBLE**; they believe that nature is the only thing that there is, so the idea of a miracle (remember, he defined a miracle as "an interference with nature by a supernatural power") would be nonsensical. If nature is the only thing that exists, then there is nothing to interfere with it.

Lewis recognises that at first glance, the most sensible way of going about the question of whether miracles happen might be to look at the historical evidence. We can look at the accounts of miracles in the Bible, or look at reports of miracles happening in places such as Lourdes, and from these reports, form a view about whether it is likely that the miracle took place. Lewis contests that this approach is entirely unhelpful as a starting point. A naturalist, Lewis points out, will look at any historical account and from it deduce that it cannot be true. This is because the naturalist believes that there is **NO SUPERNATURAL POWER THAT COULD INTERVENE IN NATURE**. The supernaturalist, on the other hand, will believe that there is a being (or more than one being) that is the cause for everything in nature, and set the natural order. The supernaturalist, therefore, will see the historical accounts of miracles to be at least possible.

Lewis has shown why an examination of the events alone is not a good way of ascertaining whether or not miracles happened, because for everyone, the question does not hinge on whether any particular historical claims are true, but rather whether you believe in the supernatural in the first place.

Laws of Nature

When we think of laws, we think, besides laws of nature, about the laws governing a particular country or group of countries. These laws are human inventions, drafted and approved in parliament. Laws can be changed, amended and overturned in the light of new thinking. Things that used to contravene laws, such as male homosexual intercourse, are now perfectly legal. Laws can also, of course, get broken, (though not without facing the possibility of there being consequences, should you get caught).

Laws of nature seem, on first appearance, to be very different from the laws of the land. They do not seem to be human inventions: it would be wrong to say that Newton invented gravity; he discovered it. Politicians, judges and others involved with law-making can, in effect, decide the law of the land; scientists can only discover what laws there are.

A Breaking of a Law of Nature?

If laws of nature have to be discovered, then perhaps they could not be broken, or if one were, it would represent an undermining of something pretty fundamental to the natural order. A law of nature is a statement of what always happens in particular circumstances. Take for example Newton's second law of motion, which states:

$$F = ma$$

(force is equal to the mass of a body, times its acceleration)

Now, if this is a law of nature, we could take this to mean:

(it is always the case that) $F = ma$

So, if a law of nature is broken, then what effectively is being claimed is that:

((it is always the case that) $F = ma$*) is not always the case*

since there is at least one case where it has been shown not to happen. Now, this is clearly a contradiction: what is always the case cannot not always be the case. In other words, if a law of nature is broken, it is contradicted; a case where the law does not hold shows that the law does not work in all cases; it is hence not a law.

So, how does the idea of a miracle as a breaking of a law of nature work? If we take Aquinas or Hume's definition of miracle, the implication seems to be that a law of nature would be broken, and then the natural order would be restored. So, according to their view, a law of nature would not be undermined by a miracle; it does not show the general law to be false. Let us explain this by using an example: the case of Jesus turning water into wine. Before the wedding in Cana, at which Jesus performed the miracle, water molecules alone could not transform to have the chemical properties that wine has: after all, alcohol is a hydrocarbon, and water has no carbon in it. Then, as Jesus performed the miracle, the normal order was broken, and wine was made from water. Afterwards, things returned to the way they were beforehand. The natural order was not done away with; it was merely suspended during the miracle.

Both Aquinas and CS Lewis's ideas of God altering the natural order are bound up with their idea of God as prior to nature. God, as creator of the world from nothing, set up the laws of nature. These laws might be absolute within the system of nature, but to their creator, they are not absolute. The example of board games is a good way to explain this. If you are playing Monopoly, you may only put houses and hotels on the squares you already own, and only if you have enough money with which to buy them. If you are playing the game, there is a set of rules that you must abide by. However, if you are just messing around with the board, you can put pieces where you like, when you like; the restrictions of what you do and when only apply when you are playing the game.

So think of nature as a bit like the Monopoly board, and the laws of nature as being like the rules. If you are part of nature, then the rules are absolute, but we can see how to God they might not be.

Are the Laws of Nature Absolute?

We have talked of a law of nature as something discovered: Newton discovered gravity; he found out that this is the way that nature always is. However, if you know anything about the paradigm shift in scientific thought that took place as a result of the work of **SIR KARL POPPER**, you will know that the idea of discovering scientific truths is one that no longer matches current scientific thinking. You might know about this as the difference between **VERIFICATION AND FALSIFICATION**, something often talked about in relation to religious language.

Karl Popper pointed out that a scientific truth is never discovered; there is no hypothesis that is not subject to the possibility of revision. Typically, a scientist will examine evidence and come up with the best possible explanation of what s/he has measured. That conclusion: that "law" can be considered true as long as there is no evidence that shows it to be false. Popper showed that not one of what we would call "the laws of nature" is incontrovertible. New evidence could come to light to show that what seemed to be the case, based on the evidence we had until now, is not true.

For example, you might boil a kettle five hundred times. It always boils at 100°C. You therefore reasonably form the conclusion that water boils at 100°C. You then climb a high mountain during your holidays. You boil water for a cup of tea. It boils at 70°C. This shows your conclusion to be false: water clearly does not always boil at 100°C. Your conclusion needs revision. After lots of research and more tests, you find that the best articulation of the "law" you discovered seems to be that under normal atmospheric pressure, pure water boils at 100°C. "Scientific laws" can only be held true until there is new evidence; **NOTHING IS EVER VERIFIED**, as new evidence could always show it to need revision; **ANY SCIENTIFIC VIEW COULD BE FALSIFIED**.

An important example of how scientific "laws" are revised is the change of perspective from the Newtonian model of Physics, to the view given to us by Quantum Mechanics. Newton's laws work for normal cases of describing what we could normally observe in the world; indeed, they are still taught on the GCSE syllabus. However, on the subatomic scale, Newtonian Physics breaks down; those laws do not work. Quantum Mechanics has shown not that Newton was wrong, but that he was not entirely right.

Science is an attempt to uncover the truth about the nature and functioning of the world, and scientists must draw their conclusions from the best available evidence. They can only draw conclusions based on what has been observed thus far.

Laws of Nature are History

Given that laws of nature can only draw conclusions based on the best evidence available at the time, **RICHARD SWINBURNE** posited that we should rethink entirely how we view them.

Naturally, we might assume that laws of nature **PRESCRIBE** what can happen. I cannot float in the air because of the amount of gravity on Earth. However, strictly, laws of nature only **DESCRIBE WHAT HAS BEEN THE CASE**; rather than prescribe what can happen in the future.

Laws of nature are conclusions based on what has been examined, which are used as predictions for what will happen.

SWINBURNE points out that in this view, laws of nature are not absolutes that are broken if a miracle happens. A miracle would not break a "law of nature" because no unchangeable fixed law has been undermined. A miracle would simply show that our understanding of

nature up until then had not included that miraculous event as a possibility; the miracle does not cohere with our past experience of nature. Perhaps, in the light of the occurrence of a miracle, our understanding of nature needs revision.

The Problem of Induction

If laws of nature are only an understanding of what has been the case, why believe that they will still work in the future? This in essence, is what philosophers call **THE PROBLEM OF INDUCTION**.

We are used to basing our understanding of what will happen on what has happened. I believe that the chair I am sitting on will not burn me, and the latte I have made will not poison me. Conversely, if I sat in the oven, it could burn me, and if I started drinking deadly nightshade, it might be the last thing I did.

This process of **INDUCTION**, drawing conclusions based on what has happened to what will happen, works well for us; we use induction all the time. The very fact that I am typing shows my faith in induction: that pressing a button on my laptop will make it work; that pressing keys will cause letters to appear on the screen; that through writing in English, my thoughts will be in some way communicated on paper.

Justification for this belief in induction is, however, pretty shaky. Why should what has taken place in the past be any guide to what will happen? We might think that the sun will always rise in the morning, but on what do we base this except the fact that it always has, and the fact that we have faith that the laws of physics and mathematics as we understand them will continue to hold?

You could say that we should believe that induction works because it always has worked in the past, but this seems highly questionable. It is understandable to say "induction has always worked, so induction will always work". Using a process of induction, though (x has always happened, therefore it always will happen), to justify induction itself, means we have to believe in induction because of induction, which is a circular justification. If someone asks you "why x?" and you say "because x", the person talking to you would not go away feeling they have received an explanation. The same would be true if we used induction to justify induction.

The best solution to the problem of induction is through a view called **RELIABILISM**. Reliabilism claims that knowledge is something we have gained through a reliable method. So provided induction happens to be reliable, then induction does provide knowledge. Similarly; provided that scientific calculations are a reliable method of finding things out, we can still form scientific conclusions.

But imagine if you witnessed a miracle; something that seemed to undermine the way science tells us the world is. Would that show that induction was not a reliable method of knowing what is likely to happen? Would it, on the other hand, show you that your eyes are deceiving you; that they are the unreliable method of discovering truth?

CONCLUSION

A discussion of nature and the laws of nature is fascinating because it cuts to the core of what events we perceive to be likely and unlikely; possible and impossible. When we examine the idea of breaking a law of nature, we discover that these "laws" are not what they seem. We can question whether evidence would ever put them in need of revision, and whether we can infer at all what will happen tomorrow, based on what has always happened.

KEY TERMS

- **NATURAL** - How something intrinsically is; how something is without human interference; being part of nature.

- **SUPERNATURAL** - Being beyond nature; above nature.

- **NATURALIST** - Generally, someone who is interested in nature. As CS Lewis defines it, this is someone who believes that nature is all that exists.

- **SUPERNATURALIST** - CS Lewis's term; someone who believes that there is a supernatural, as well as natural, aspect to the world.

- **VERIFICATION** - Showing something to be true.

- **FALSIFICATION** - Showing something to be false.

- **INDUCTION** - Inferring, based on what has happened, what will happen in the future.

- **RELIABILISM** - The view that we can know things if and only if we obtain them using a reliable method.

SELF-ASSESSMENT QUESTIONS

1. Does it make sense to talk of a law of nature being broken?

2. Does what has happened provide a good guide for what will happen?

3. Does what has happened provide a reason for thinking that certain things could never happen?

FURTHER READING

- **CLACK, B & CLACK, BR** - The Philosophy of Religion: A Critical Introduction, 2nd ed. Polity Press, 2008, pp. 142-144; pp. 146-147

- **COLE, P** - Philosophy of Religion, 2nd ed. Hodder Murray, 2009, pp. 61-62

- **LEWIS, CS** - Miracles, Collins, 1947, especially Ch. 8

- **POXON, B** - A2 Philosophy: Revision Guide for OCR, PushMe Press, 2013, pp. 78-80

- **SWINBURNE, R** - The Existence of God, 3rd ed. OUP, 2004, Ch. 12

- **WARD, K** - The Big Questions in Science and Religion, Templeton Foundation Press, 2008, Ch. 4

The Role of Miracles Within Religion

At the heart of many religions are stories of miracles. Thinking for example of the Jewish tradition, we remember the stories of manna being provided to the people of Israel in the wilderness, or the parting of the Red Sea, where the Jews were saved from the Egyptians. These tremendous tales are passed on through the generations, and are often the first things children learn as part of an induction into their religion, or the religions of others. Key narratives and celebrations in a religious tradition are often underpinned by tales of the miraculous.

Some examples:

HANUKKAH (Judaism)

Commemoration	Miracle
An eight-branched candlestick called a Menorah is lit, one light each night, for eight nights.	A group of Jews called the Maccabees rebelled against the Syrian King Antiochus, who instructed the Jews to worship Greek Gods. They managed to defend the temple, although everywhere else was razed to the ground. They set about cleaning and restoring the temple, which took eight days. They found only a little bit of oil; it should have been the case that the oil ran out, and their task remained unfinished, but that little bit of oil lasted for eight whole days, which allowed them to defend and restore the temple.

PASSOVER (Judaism)

Commemoration	Miracle
As well as special services at temple, a special meal of lamb and bitter herbs is eaten, to commemorate the miracle.	The Israelites were living as slaves in Egypt. Moses, who was raised in the Egyptian royal household, but who was Jewish, petitioned Pharaoh a number of times to let the Israelites go. When he refused, God sent plague after plague on Egypt, the culmination of which was when God killed the first-born son of each family, except those that sacrificed a lamb, and smeared the blood onto the lintel of their door. The plague thus "passed over" the houses of the Israelites, and their first-born sons were saved.

EASTER (Christianity)

Commemoration	Miracle
In many churches, services are held in the middle of the night and finish at dawn, to symbolise the resurrection; Jesus overcoming death.	Holy Week commemorates the journey of Christ to his death on the cross, and resurrection three days later on Easter Day. Jesus was betrayed by one of his disciples, Judas, and was handed to the Romans. Jesus was tried for blasphemy, as he said he was King of the Jews. He was crucified with two common criminals, one at his left, and one at his right. He died, and, as Christian teaching has it, the sky went dark for three hours. On the third day after his death, Jesus' women followers went to his tomb to tend his grave, and found it empty. He was resurrected from the dead. He made a number of appearances to his Disciples, before ascending into heaven.

HOLI (Hinduism)

Commemoration	Miracle
This is the spring festival, where there is a celebration of spring overcoming winter, and good overcoming evil. Typically, it is celebrated by large crowds dancing as well as throwing lots of coloured powder over each other. Practical jokes are played and bonfires are lit to symbolise good triumphing over evil.	Prahlad was a prince, whose father, the King, wanted everyone to worship him, not a deity. Little Prahlad refused, and continued instead to worship Lord Vishnu. The King was furious and conspired with his sister Holika, to kill Prahlad. Holika was thought to have a special power of being able to resist fire, and sat the little boy on her lap, whilst she sat on a bonfire. But she was using her powers for evil, not for good, and so she was consumed by the flames, and little Prahlad was saved.

What is Important About These Miracles?

In the Hindu tradition, it is common to focus not on the veracity of the event itself, but on its **RELIGIOUS SIGNIFICANCE**. Of course, if Holika caught on fire, but Prahlad, who was sitting on her knee, emerged unscathed, nature appears not to be functioning as it normally would. The event does seem to contain a breach or disturbance in nature, though it is not mentioned in the story that this is anything to do with a direct intervention by a deity (we might, though, assume that it has something to do with Lord Vishnu, as Prahlad worshipped him and was saved). This is not, however, what is taken from the story. The important aspect of the story in the Hindu tradition is that it shows that good triumphs over evil. It is not just coincidence that Holi is celebrated in spring, when new growth happens and the barrenness of winter is defeated. Arguably, the focus for understanding the miracle of Prahlad and Holika is entirely on the meaning of the event, and not about whether it actually happened.

As with many Jewish stories, not just stories of miracles, at the centre of our understanding should be Jewish identity as a people chosen by God. Of fundamental importance are two questions: "What does it mean to be Jewish?" and "What is the Jewish relationship with God?" The two miracles explained above provide answers to these two questions. The miracle of the oil in the temple lamp shows that there is hope for the Jewish people, even in times of great darkness; as it says in Isaiah 9:2 "the people that walked in darkness have seen a great light". In this miracle story, the Jews are, as they so frequently are in the Old Testament, an exiled people; they are living under someone else's rule in a foreign land. Those who remain faithful to God and the temple are given hope. This miracle is not dramatic; at best it bends a law of nature. Arguably, if it were understood to just be about the oil in the temple lamp not going out, it would be a small miracle indeed. It is the significance for the Jewish people in a time of great struggle that makes the miracle special and worthy of commemoration.

The Passover is an event on a wholly different scale, and is clearly "an event of an extraordinary kind". A sacrifice of a lamb and its blood on the lintel saves the first-born sons in Jewish households, whilst every first-born son of Egypt dies. Again, though, without the religious significance in this event, we only have a partial understanding of what is really going on. This event is as much about the fact that the Jews are preserved by God; they are the chosen people. It also links the Jewish people in Egypt with the story of Abraham in Genesis, where Abraham is willing to sacrifice his son on God's command, but God stops him, and tells him to sacrifice a young ram instead. Just as in the story of Abraham, the first-born here are saved because of a sacrifice God instructs them to make. The Passover story answers the two questions we posed earlier: to be Jewish is to be part of a people who are the inheritors of Abraham's legacy; the Jewish relationship with God is that He guides and protects His chosen people. To understand this event purely for its unusual nature would be partial; it is only when considered for its religious significance that it is fully comprehended.

Miraculous Events: Especially Important in the Christian Tradition?

It could be argued that in the case of the other miracles we have examined in this chapter (Hanukkah, Passover and Holi), the religious significance of these events is enough to express their importance to the tradition. This is less clear with some of the central miracles in Christianity, such as the resurrection of Jesus, because it seems that it is on these miraculous events that Christianity is centred, and arguably on which the validity of it as a world view is hinged.

If we think about the Christian tradition, belief in a miracle lies at its very centre; namely the miraculous resurrection of Christ three days after his death. The Creed, the statement of belief made by Christians, says that "on the third day he [Jesus] rose from the dead, ascended into heaven, and sits on the right hand of God, the Father Almighty". It seems that especially for Christianity, miracles are not simply a part of the story, they are at the heart of the faith; to be a Christian is to believe that "Christ has died, Christ is risen, Christ will come again".

Just as with the other miracles discussed, understanding the death and resurrection of Christ would be meaningless if its significance in the context of a religious tradition were not understood. The death and resurrection should be understood to show something about the superfluity of God's love, that so great a sacrifice should be made for mankind. As it says in John 3: "God so loved the world that He gave his only begotten son that whosoever believes in him should not perish, but have everlasting life. For God sent not His son into the world to condemn the world, but that the world through Him might be saved."

However, religious significance is arguably not enough here, because if the miracle did not occur, if God did not send His son, then perhaps His great love for mankind has not been shown? It is clear that the Gospels intend to persuade us of the message of Jesus through the use of the stories of miracles. As it says in John 20:30-31: "These things are written, that you may believe … and in believing have eternal life in His name."

More than this, it is believed by Christians that it is through Jesus' death and resurrection that the salvation of the world is possible. A traditional Latin prayer makes clear the connection:

> Salvator mundi, salva nos,
> qui per crucem et sanguinem redemisti nos, auxiliare nobis, te de precamur, Deus noster.
> O Saviour of the world, save us,
> who by thy cross and blood hast redeemed us, help us, we pray thee, O Lord our God.

It is clear that the crucifixion is the means by which the redemption of mankind can be achieved. So what if the crucifixion and resurrection never happened? Is mankind saved?

CONCLUSION

We have found that miracles form an important part of the narratives of many religions. Although many of these events are extraordinary, and may seem to break laws of nature, often the religious significance is what gives the narrative its richness and its importance. Arguably, it is more important in the Christian tradition that the miracles are not just symbolic, but that they actually happened; unlike the other faiths we have examined, miracles are at the very centre of the Christian faith. Perhaps this can explain why so much discussion of the nature and possibility of miracles happens within the Christian tradition; whether miracles happen or not is of fundamental importance to the faith.

KEY TERMS

- **RELIGIOUS NARRATIVE** - Stories within a religious context, or indeed the story, the central concepts, ideas, or world view that is encompassed by that religion.

- **RELIGIOUS TRADITION** - A combination of the narratives, core beliefs, religious thinking and practice that together creates a certain tradition.

- **RELIGIOUS SIGNIFICANCE** - Importance within a certain religious context, perhaps the illumination of truths in certain narratives, or an addition of a new concept within a certain tradition.

SELF-ASSESSMENT QUESTIONS

1. Which of the definitions from the first Chapter best reflects the role that miracles have within religion?

2. Which of the definitions from the first Chapter worst reflects the role that miracles have within religion?

3. Is the truth of miraculous accounts more important in Christianity? Why not?

FURTHER READING

*   **COLE, P** - Philosophy of Religion, 2nd ed. Hodder Murray, 2009, pp. 69-70

*   **DAVIES, B** - An Introduction to the Philosophy of Religion, 3rd ed. OUP, 2004, pp. 257-259

*   **VARDY, P** - The Puzzle of God, 2nd ed. Fount, 1999, pp. 213-215

A List of Biblical Miracles

There are lots of miracles that could be listed here. In the Synoptic Gospels, especially, there are lots of miracle accounts, many of which are similar in their nature. For example, there are lots of healings, some of similar diseases. Therefore, listed below is a small selection of the miracles presented in the Bible.

OLD TESTAMENT

REFERENCE	EVENT	QUOTATIONS
Exodus 14:21-31	God parts the Red Sea, enabling the safe passage of the Israelites out of Egypt.	Ex 14:31 And when the Israelites saw the mighty hand of the Lord displayed against the Egyptians, the people feared the Lord and put their trust in him and in Moses his servant.
Joshua 10:12-14	Joshua asks God to make the sun stop still in the sky, and it did until his nation had won the battle against its enemies.	Josh 10:13 So the sun stood still, and the moon stopped, till the nation avenged itself on its enemies, as it is written in the Book of Jashar. The sun stopped in the middle of the sky and delayed going down about a full day.

REFERENCE	EVENT	QUOTATIONS
Exodus 16	*The Israelites are starving in the wilderness, and God rains down manna (bread) from heaven.*	*Ex 16:4 In this way I will test them and see whether they will follow my instructions. On the sixth day they are to prepare what they bring in, and that is to be twice as much as they gather on the other days.*
Daniel 6	*Daniel is cast into the lions' den by King Darius. The King challenges Daniel that God should save him. That night, the King cannot sleep, and when he goes to check on Daniel, he has indeed not been eaten. The King is overjoyed and comes to belief in God.*	*Dan 6:27 For he is the living God and he endures forever; his kingdom will not be destroyed, his dominion will never end. He rescues and he saves; he performs signs and wonders in the heavens and on the earth. He has rescued Daniel from the power of the lions.*

THE GOSPELS

REFERENCE	EVENT	QUOTATIONS
John 2:1-11	*Jesus turns water into wine at a wedding in Cana.*	*John 2:11 What Jesus did here in Cana of Galilee was the first of the signs through which he revealed his glory; and his disciples believed in him.*
Matthew 8:1-4 **Mark 1:40-45** **Luke 5:12-16**	*Jesus cures a man of leprosy.*	*Mark 1:43-45 Jesus sent him away at once with a strong warning: "See that you don't tell this to anyone. But go, show yourself to the priest and offer the sacrifices that Moses commanded for your cleansing, as a testimony to them." Instead he went out and began to talk freely, spreading the news. As a result, Jesus could no longer enter a town openly but stayed outside in lonely places. Yet the people still came to him from everywhere.*

REFERENCE	EVENT	QUOTATIONS
Matthew 8:23-27 **Mark 4:35-41** **Luke 8:22-25**	*Jesus calms the storm.*	*Mark 4:39-41 He got up, rebuked the wind and said to the waves, "Quiet! Be still!" Then the wind died down and it was completely calm.* *He said to his disciples, "Why are you so afraid? Do you still have no faith?" They were terrified and asked each other, "Who is this? Even the wind and the waves obey him!"*
Matthew 14:13-21 **Mark 6:31-34** **Luke 9:10-17** **John 6:5-15**	*Jesus feeds the five thousand.*	*Luke 9:16-17 Taking the five loaves and the two fish and looking up to heaven, he gave thanks and broke them. Then he gave them to the disciples to distribute to the people. They all ate and were satisfied, and the disciples picked up twelve basketfuls of broken pieces that were left over.*

REFERENCE	EVENT	QUOTATIONS
Matthew 9:18-26 **Mark 5:21-43** **Luke 8:40-56**	*Jesus cures Jairus's/the synagogue leader's daughter.*	*Matt 9:23-26 When Jesus entered the synagogue leader's house and saw the noisy crowd and people playing pipes, he said, "Go away. The girl is not dead but asleep." But they laughed at him. After the crowd had been put outside, he went in and took the girl by the hand, and she got up. News of this spread through all that region.*
Matthew 17:14-21 **Mark 9:14-29** **Luke 9:37-49**	*Jesus exorcises a boy who is possessed by a demon.*	*Luke 9:42 The demon threw him to the ground in a convulsion. But Jesus rebuked the impure spirit, healed the boy and gave him back to his father. And they were all amazed at the greatness of God.*

MIRACLES AS PRESENTED IN JOHN'S GOSPEL

The presentation of the stories of miracles in John's Gospel is very different to that of the Synoptic Gospels (that is Matthew, Mark and Luke). For a start, there are many more miracles in the Synoptic Gospels. Secondly, the purpose of these narratives seems to be completely different.

If you have ever had cause to study one or more of the Gospels, you will know that Matthew, Mark and Luke **SHARE A COMMON SOURCE**, known as "Q", which is short for the German "Quelle", which means "source". John was written later, probably around 100AD, and although there are many similarities between John and the other three Gospels, John is both more theologically developed, and clearly too has a number of influences, including not only Hebrew thought, but also Greek philosophy.

The Greek word most used in the Synoptic Gospels to describe miracles is δύναμις (dynamis). This word means **GREAT POWER**. Miracles in these Gospels, therefore, are presented as tremendous acts of power. They demonstrate Jesus' power over nature; his divine capacity to circumvent the natural order of things. The idea of a miracle as δύναμις (dynamis), therefore, is one that is roughly consistent with Aquinas's or CS Lewis's view. These miracles show a supernatural being with power over nature: a being with the capacity to, perhaps, break laws of nature, but certainly to, as CS Lewis says, "interfere" in nature.

In John, δύναμις (dynamis) is not the word used to talk of the miraculous. Rather than emphasising divine potency, John chooses to emphasise the significance of the events. The word used in John is σημεῖον (semeion), which means **SIGN**. We can see immediately that this coheres with Tillich's view, that miracles are "sign-events". John's presentations of these signs are infused with theological significance. In fact, were you to look at these miracles simply as stories about Jesus' divine power, you would be missing much of what was written.

Even the number of signs that John includes could be seen to be symbolic. As we know, in Genesis the world is said to be created in seven days. You may think that this is seven days because the week has seven days, but there is more to it than that. Seven is a Jewish number of perfection, or completeness. So it takes seven days for the universe to be complete in Genesis. Similarly, there are seven signs in John's Gospel. You could take this to mean that at the end of the seventh sign, Jesus' work on Earth is completed. The last miracle Jesus performs is the raising of Lazarus. Jesus raising Lazarus a numbered of days after his death is a clear foreshadowing of Jesus' own death and resurrection. It is therefore after this event that the "Book of Signs", as **C DODD** calls it, is complete, and the time comes for Jesus to be betrayed into the hands of his enemies. This idea of completeness might be further reflected in the words of Jesus as he dies on the cross. In the Gospel of John, Jesus' last words are simply "it is finished".

It is important not to start thinking that the miracles in the Synoptic Gospels fall under one definition, and that miracles in John fall under another. **JOHN MARSH**, an important scholar of John's Gospel, points out that in the light of John's signs, we can understand the importance of religious significance in the miracles from the other Gospels. So, according to Marsh, the miracle narratives, including those not in John, can all be interpreted as religiously significant events.

So perhaps, the definitions that fit best with the biblical depictions of miracles, and especially John's "signs", are Tillich's and Swinburne's, namely those that emphasise the religious significance of the event, unlike Hume, Aquinas and CS Lewis, but also recognise that these are divine events, unlike RF Holland.

A CLOSER READING OF JOHN'S SIGNS

There is a lot that could be, and indeed has been, said about the seven signs in John's Gospel. For the purposes of this book we will focus here only on three, and will examine the most important themes.

Water into Wine: John 2:1-11

On the third day a wedding took place at Cana in Galilee. Jesus' mother was there, and Jesus and his disciples had also been invited to the wedding. When the wine was gone, Jesus' mother said to him, "They have no more wine." "Woman, why do you involve me?" Jesus replied. "My hour has not yet come." His mother said to the servants, "Do whatever he tells you." Nearby stood six stone water jars, the kind used by the Jews for ceremonial washing, each holding from eighty to a hundred and twenty litres. Jesus said to the servants, "Fill the jars with water"; so they filled them to the brim. Then he told them, "Now draw some out and take it to the master of the banquet." They did so, and the master of the banquet tasted the water that had been turned into wine. He did not realise where it had come from, though the servants who had drawn the water knew. Then he called the bridegroom aside and said, "Everyone brings out the choice wine first and then the cheaper wine after the guests have had too much to drink; but you have saved the best till now." What Jesus did here in Cana of Galilee was the first of the signs through which he revealed his glory; and his disciples believed in him.

This event is often read more like a magic trick than a sign that is intended to point to religious significance, but yet this text is a rich tapestry of religious meaning. As **MARSH** notes, the fact that the event occurs on the "third day" both links what has happened in the days before, where Jesus calls his disciples, and allows us to look forward. As **CK BARRETT** also notes, the "third day" is an allusion to the third day after Jesus' death; his resurrection. This sign marks the beginning of Jesus' ministry; with the crucifixion and resurrection as the inescapable conclusion.

The context for this miracle is a wedding, and this is itself symbolic. In the Old Testament, there is an image that is frequently used of Yahweh (God) being the bridegroom of Israel; the idea that God and Israel are bound to one another. To place Jesus in the context of a wedding is to make a claim about who Jesus is, namely a **CHRISTOLOGICAL** claim; Jesus is perhaps to be seen as the new bridegroom of Israel.

CK BARRETT and **BULTMANN** both note that central to this sign is the idea that Judaism needs reviving, fulfilling, and it is Jesus who does this. We are told that the wine had run out: **CK BARRETT** argues that the fact this is made clear suggests emptiness in Judaism, a need for revival. Jesus is brought six empty vessels, and tells the servant to fill them with water. Again, emptiness is mentioned, but the fact that there are six is also important. In Judaism, seven is the number of completeness. The fact that there are only six vessels has been taken by some to indicate the incompleteness of Judaism. Moreover, these were the pots that Jews used for ceremonial washing, which might point to the fact that Jewish ritual was no longer enough. The water might refer to what happened in the chapter before, where John the Baptist baptises with water alone but

Jesus is one who baptises with water and the Holy Spirit. The water is important, but it is incomplete. As **MARSH** notes, this sign shows Jesus as one with **TRANSFORMATIVE POWER**; he can transform water into wine; he can transform Judaism. Interestingly, the sign records no specific action by Jesus; it is by his words that the event occurs. This could be linked to the Genesis 1 creation myth, where God speaks the world into existence by saying "let there be light"; this would link Jesus' actions with God's creative power.

At the end of the narrative, we are made aware that this is not intended as a showing of divine power, but rather that it is an event intended to show who Jesus is. His disciples believe in him as a result of him "show[ing] his glory"; this event is about who Jesus is.

The Feeding of the Five Thousand: John 6:1-15

Some time after this, Jesus crossed to the far shore of the Sea of Galilee (that is, the Sea of Tiberias), and a great crowd of people followed him because they saw the signs he had performed by healing those who were ill. Then Jesus went up on a mountainside and sat down with his disciples. The Jewish Passover Festival was near. When Jesus looked up and saw a great crowd coming towards him, he said to Philip, "Where shall we buy bread for these people to eat?" He asked this only to test him, for he already had in mind what he was going to do. Philip answered him, "It would take more than half a year's wages to buy enough bread for each one to have a bite!" Another of his disciples, Andrew, Simon Peter's brother, spoke up, "Here is a boy with five small barley loaves and two small fish, but how far will they go among so many?" Jesus said, "Make the people sit down." There was plenty of grass in that place, and they sat down (about five thousand men were there). Jesus then took the loaves, gave thanks, and distributed to those who were seated as much as they wanted. He did the same with the fish.

When they had all had enough to eat, he said to his disciples, "Gather the pieces that are left over. Let nothing be wasted." So they gathered them and filled twelve baskets with the pieces of the five barley loaves left over by those who had eaten. After the people saw the sign Jesus performed, they began to say, "Surely this is the Prophet who is to come into the world." Jesus, knowing that they intended to come and make him king by force, withdrew again to a mountain by himself.

Food is a fundamental need; it is what allows us to stay alive. The fact that the sign of the feeding of the five thousand is followed in John by Jesus teaching that he is "the Bread of Life" therefore gives a very strong message. Just as earthly bread allows us to stay alive, so Jesus is the means by which eternal life is achieved.

MARTYN noted that this sign, taking place on a mountain, could be a repetition of the miracle in the time of Moses, where God rained down manna (bread) from heaven. The feeding of the five thousand could also have the significance of God being a provider for Jews in times of struggle. In Exodus, Moses leads the Jews away from slavery in the land of Egypt. In the time of Jesus, Jews were living under another foreign power; the Romans.

There is also a clear foreshadowing of the **LAST SUPPER** here, with Jesus breaking bread and sharing it amongst his followers. Moreover, the actions of Jesus at the Last Supper have become central to Christian Eucharistic ritual, which is also clearly alluded to.

Afterwards, twelve baskets of crumbs are gathered up. Some have suggested that this is just a pragmatic wish not to waste food, but others have claimed that it goes deeper than this. Perhaps this symbolises a gathering of Christian disciples: Jesus refers to himself as "the good shepherd" later on in the Gospel, and in the Old Testament, we hear the prophecy that "He shall feed his flock like a shepherd". Perhaps the gathering refers not just generally to Christian disciples; maybe the fact that there are twelve baskets is important. One plausible suggestion is that it could mean that he will gather the twelve tribes of Israel.

As **C DODD** puts it, it is clear that this event is truly miraculous, but also that it is much more than just miraculous; it has a deep symbolic level as well.

The Raising of Lazarus: John 11:1-44

Now a man named Lazarus was ill. He was from Bethany, the village of Mary and her sister Martha ... So the sisters sent word to Jesus, "Lord, the one you love is ill." When he heard this, Jesus said, "This illness will not end in death. No, it is for God's glory so that God's Son may be glorified through it." Now Jesus loved Martha and her sister and Lazarus. So when he heard that Lazarus was ill, he stayed where he was two more days, and then he said to his disciples, "Let us go back to Judea." "But Rabbi," they said, "a short while ago the Jews there tried to stone you, and yet you are going back?" Jesus answered, "Are there not twelve hours of daylight? Anyone who walks in the day-time will not stumble, for they see by this world's light. It is when a person walks at night that they stumble, for they have no light." After he had said this, he went on to tell them, "Our friend Lazarus has fallen asleep; but I am going there to wake him up." His disciples replied, "Lord, if he sleeps, he will get better." Jesus had been speaking of his death, but his disciples thought he meant natural sleep. So then he told them plainly, "Lazarus is dead, and for your sake I am glad I was not there, so that you may believe. But let us go to him." ...

On his arrival, Jesus found that Lazarus had already been in the tomb for four days ... When Martha heard that Jesus was coming, she went out to meet him, but Mary stayed at home. "Lord," Martha said to Jesus, "if you had been here, my brother would not have died. But I know that even now God will give you whatever you ask." Jesus said to her, "Your brother will rise again." Martha answered, "I know he will rise again in the resurrection at the last day." Jesus said to her, "I am the resurrection and the life. The one who believes in me will live, even though they die; and whoever lives by believing in me will never die. Do you believe this?" "Yes, Lord," she replied, "I believe that you are the Messiah, the Son of God, who is to come into the world." After she had said this, she went back and called her sister Mary aside. "The Teacher is here," she said, "and is asking for you." When Mary heard this, she got up quickly and went to him. Now Jesus had not yet entered the village, but was still at the place where Martha had met him. When the Jews who had been with Mary in the house, comforting her, noticed how quickly she got up and went out, they followed her, supposing she was going to the tomb to mourn there. When Mary reached the place where Jesus was and saw him, she fell at his feet and said, "Lord, if you had been here, my brother would not have died." When Jesus saw her *weeping, and the Jews who had come along with her also weeping, he was deeply moved in spirit and troubled. "Where have you laid him?" he asked. "Come and see, Lord," they replied. Jesus wept. Then the Jews said, "See how he loved him!" But some of them said, "Could not he who opened the eyes of the blind man have kept this man from dying?"*

Jesus, once more deeply moved, came to the tomb. It was a cave with a stone laid across the entrance. "Take away the stone," he said. "But, Lord," said Martha, the sister of the dead man, "by this time there is a bad odour, for he has been there four days." Then Jesus said, "Did I not tell you that if you believe, you will see the glory of God?" So they took away the stone. Then Jesus looked up and said, "Father, I thank you that you have heard me. I knew that you always hear me, but I said this for the benefit of the people standing here, that they may believe that you sent me." When he had said this, Jesus called in a loud voice, "Lazarus, come out!" The dead man came out, his hands and feet wrapped with strips of linen, and a cloth round his face. Jesus said to them, "Take off the grave clothes and let him go."

A lot of the significance of this sign comes from its context. As an isolated story, it is impressive as a miraculous event - raising someone from the dead would fall under anyone's definition of a miracle - but in the context it has within the Gospel, it also has other significance. This is the last sign that Jesus performs; his crucifixion is near, and we can see that Jesus is in danger, as his disciples warn him not to go to Judea; he was nearly stoned to death the last time he went there.

Some of Jesus' behaviour in this sign is strange to say the least. We are told that Jesus loved Mary, Martha and Lazarus, yet when he hears that Lazarus is ill, he seems to sit tight and wait until he is dead. As we see from what both sisters say to him, they are aware that had Jesus come sooner, their brother need never have died. What Jesus says to his disciples here is the key: "Lazarus is dead, and for your sake I am glad I was not there, so that you may believe." In other words, this is a sign event: for the disciples' sake, Jesus is glad, because then they will believe. The delay, as **CK BARRETT** notes, is deliberate, so God may be glorified.

MARSH points out that Jesus' raising Lazarus from the dead is not a case of reviving him from suspended animation. The fact that Lazarus has been in the tomb for four days confirms that he really is dead. According to Jewish tradition, the soul would have left the body by now. Jesus, as **FENTON** notes, is overthrowing the last enemy: Jesus has power over death. We can see this in what he says to Martha. Martha, like a good Jewish girl, believes that the resurrection will be on the Last Day. Jesus says to her "I am the Resurrection and the Life. The one who believes in me will live, even though they die; and whoever lives by believing in me will never die." Jesus does not merely triumph over death in the resurrection of Lazarus; he promises eternal life to all his believers.

CONCLUSION

From this brief exploration of three of the signs in John's Gospel, it is clear that although there is a lot about each of these events that is extraordinary, even contrary to nature, this is not all that is going on. Some understanding of the event comes from understanding it as an extraordinary occurrence, but so much of the symbolic content is lost if we fail to understand these events as signs.

KEY TERMS

- **SYNOPTIC GOSPELS** - The Gospels of Matthew, Mark and Luke, which were written before John, and share a common source.

- **Q** - Short for **"QUELLE"**, which in German means "source"; "Q" is the common source that the Synoptic Gospels share.

- **DYNAMIS** - Greek, meaning "power". This is the word used to describe the miracles in the Synoptic Gospels.

- **SEMEION** - Greek, meaning "sign". This is the word used to describe the miracles in John.

SELF-ASSESSMENT QUESTIONS

1. In what way are the accounts of miracles in John different from the other Gospels?

2. Which definition of miracle accords best with the sign narratives in John?

3. Read the narrative of "The Feeding of the Five Thousand", including what follows on "The Bread of Life". Then, read "The Feeding of the Five Thousand" in one of the Synoptic Gospels. How are they different?

FURTHER READING

- **MARSH, J** - Saint John, 2nd ed. Penguin, 1968, pp. 59-66

- **BARRETT, CK** - The Gospel According to Saint John, 2nd ed. SPCK, 2009, Chapters 4, 12 and 22

Reports of Miracles at Lourdes

A CASE STUDY

When thinking of miracles, our first thought is perhaps the miracles of Jesus. These were events that, if they took place, did so in a country far away, around 2,000 years ago, and were witnessed by people long dead. But reports of miracles continue to this day, and some sites are so reputed for their miraculous events that they become centres of pilgrimage for millions.

LOURDES, in France, is one such place. In 1858, a 14-year-old girl called **BERNADETTE SOUBIROUS** reportedly had a series of visions of the Virgin Mary in a cave. Initially, Bernadette did not know who this lady, dressed in white with a blue sash and yellow roses on her feet, was. After a while, the lady identified herself as "The Immaculate Conception", a term that the Pope had only given to Mary four years earlier, and which Bernadette would not have heard of, especially as she spoke an obscure dialect. The lady instructed Bernadette to dig to a spring and drink from it. After her fourth attempt, clear water flowed, and still flows to this day. Many people thought that Bernadette was mad, with her seemingly neurotic desire to keep visiting this cave and dig in the dirt; in fact, there was a time at which she was nearly locked up. But the crowds started to build up around the well, curious to see whether Bernadette was unstable or inspired by the divine. Reports of **MIRACULOUS HEALINGS** started to come, and despite much scepticism by many, especially those in the Roman Catholic Church, the validity of what she had been saying started to become apparent to them, and people started petitioning the Church to build a shrine there.

Now, millions of pilgrims visit the cave to place their hands on the rock, take water from the spring and pray to the Virgin Mary. Many of those who visit are hoping for a cure. There have been so many claims of miracles that a special bureau has been set up to handle them. Many more still are reticent to make an official claim that a miracle took place, some for fear of publicity; some for fear of trivialising such an important event in their lives.

A Wary Church

Surprisingly perhaps, especially to those who suspect that religious believers might be keen to believe miraculous events, The Roman Catholic Church has been extremely reticent to verify claims of miracles. The Lourdes Medical Bureau was set up to process and investigate claims of the miraculous. Since Bernadette's visions, there have been **AROUND SEVEN THOUSAND CLAIMS OF MIRACLES**, and only sixty-eight have been formally accepted as such by the Roman Catholic Church; that is just under 1% of the claims.

Each person making a claim that a miracle has taken place files an official petition, which is then reviewed by the doctors at the Medical Bureau. Healings must have been instant as well as permanent. Medical tests may be performed, to ensure that the cure has in fact taken place. It is then presented to an international medical board, which has major figures in medicine from around the world, some of whom are agnostics or atheists. Once the doctors are happy that the claim is supported by medical evidence, it is then referred to the bishop. A very few of these cases are then proclaimed to have been miraculous.

Lourdes' Most Recent Miracle

In October 2012, Lourdes announced its 68th miracle. **SISTER LUIGINA TRAVERSO** from Casale Monferrato in Italy had a paralysed leg since the age of 30. She had numerous operations on her spine; none of them worked. She ended up confined to her bed. In 1965, she visited Lourdes, and reportedly felt a great warming sensation as well as feeling blessed. She found herself able to stand, and felt the pain go away. Sister Luigina then visited the Medical Bureau twice in two years. After the second visit, they agreed to open a case on her. The Medical Board discussed her case in 1966, 1984 and 2010, and new medical examinations were used to ensure that they were using the most up-to-date scientific evidence available. In 2011, the Medical Board concluded that the healing was inexplicable, given current scientific knowledge. The case was then referred to Sister Luigina's bishop, and on 11 October, 2012, her healing was finally declared a miracle.

You can see from this case the Church's hesitancy in accepting the healing as a miracle. The process of verification took 47 years in all, and the Medical Board met three times over a period of 44 years to decide whether her case was truly inexplicable. This shows that, contrary to what many might think, the Roman Catholic Church does not verify miracles lightly.

Other Explanations

It might be said that many or even all of the supposed cures at Lourdes could be explained by the **PLACEBO EFFECT**. The word "placebo" comes from the Latin, meaning "I will please", and names a cure that takes place because a patient believes that they are being treated. It has been demonstrated that being given drugs in branded packaging actually makes them more effective at fighting pain, compared to their own-brand rivals. This is not because branded painkillers are any different to the paracetamol and ibuprofen in the other packaging, but because the branding makes us believe they will be more effective, which in turn makes them more effective. In addition, experiments by psychologist Irving Kirsch has shown that sugar pills are 80% as effective as Prozac at alleviating the symptoms of depression, so long as the patients believe that they are taking Prozac.

It has therefore been quite well demonstrated that what a patient believes can affect their cure. Perhaps the healing waters are similar to the sugar pill; the water heals because patients believe that it will. After all, nearly all visitors to Lourdes are already believing Roman Catholics, and if someone goes to Lourdes hoping for a cure, that seems to imply already that they have a belief that that sort of thing is possible.

"Your Faith Has Healed You"

Those who believe that the shrine at Lourdes can provide miraculous cures might contest this. They could argue that the placebo effect does not mean that no miracle has taken place. The idea that a great faith could heal is by no means a new one. When Jesus is on his way to heal Jairus's daughter, a woman, who hopes to be healed, touches Jesus' cloak. She is healed, and Jesus says to her, "**DAUGHTER, YOUR FAITH HAS HEALED YOU**. Go in peace and be freed from your suffering." (Mark 5:34) Another example of this is when Jesus comes across a blind man, who wants to see again. "Jesus said to him, 'Receive your sight; your faith has healed you.' Immediately he received his sight and followed Jesus, praising God. When all the people saw it, they also praised God." (Luke 18:42-43) The Bible does claim that **FAITH CAN**

HEAL; the placebo effect does not, therefore, overcome the possibility of the miraculous.

KEY TERMS

- **LOURDES MEDICAL BUREAU** - A group of medics who work at Lourdes, and sift through claims of the miraculous, to find what might be true cases of miracle cures.

- **LOURDES INTERNATIONAL MEDICAL BOARD** - A group of internationally recognised doctors, including agnostics and atheists, who meet to discuss cases put forward by the Medical Bureau, to establish whether there is a known medical explanation for cures that reportedly happened at Lourdes.

- **PLACEBO EFFECT** - Healing that takes place when the patient beliefs that the cure is working, or will work. Sugar pills, if a patient believes them to be the drugs they need, can have some effect in curing them.

SELF-ASSESSMENT QUESTIONS

1. Does the reticence of the Roman Catholic Church to verify miracles make those it does verify more probable?

2. Which of the definitions best describes the miracles reported to happen at Lourdes?

3. Does the placebo effect provide a challenge to the veracity of the miraculous claims at Lourdes?

Credulity and Credibility

One of the most interesting things about the topic of miracles is that it gets to the heart of some big questions in **EPISTEMOLOGY**, namely the philosophical questions surrounding knowledge and how it is acquired. Miracles are incredible events, both in the sense of being extraordinary, as well as in the literal sense of being in-credible; they are not believable. If I told you that the content of my cup was a latte, you would probably find that credible. If I told you that the cup contained water that had miraculously been turned into wine, you would react differently. Miraculous events are, by their very nature, not easily believed. If they were run-of-the-mill events, they would not be miraculous. This makes them a good springboard for a discussion of what makes something, or someone, credible.

"Credere" is the Latin verb meaning "to believe". From it, we get a number of our words to do with believing. There is **CREED**, which is a statement of belief, most frequently used in religious settings; **CREDIBLE**, which describes something believable; and **CREDULITY**, which describes how believing a person is. Nowadays, "credulous" has come to be used more frequently in a pejorative way, to describe someone who believes too readily. For the purposes of our discussion, though, I am using it in its neutral sense to describe the state of believing in a person. So, a miracle might be **INCREDIBLE**, and people hearing reports of a miracle might be **INCREDULOUS**, i.e. they don't believe the reports.

We are looking now at both credibility (what makes people or events believable or unbelievable) and credulity (what things we tend to be credulous or incredulous about ourselves).

WHAT MAKES A REPORT CREDIBLE?

Let us begin by considering the testimony that other people give us. We use other people's reports every single day in order to find things out about the world. From the moment the radio wakes you in the morning, you are relying on the accounts that others give you. Do you visit war zones or terrorist cells to find out what's going on in the world? Do you have your own meteorological system in your garden so you can find out the weather? No, you rely on accounts given to you. As John Donne told us: "No man is an island": we are dependent on one another, and have to trust what other people say.

Having said this, just because we often rely on what others tell us, that does not mean that we always believe others, or that we should believe others. Whether we give credence to what they say depends, really, on two things: who they are and what they are claiming.

Who Are They?

Consider the following people:

- Your parent

- Your sibling

- Your close friend

- Your teacher

- Someone you don't know, but who has a field of expertise

- Someone you know to be very gullible

- Someone you don't know at all

- Someone with problems with addiction to drugs or alcohol

If you were to put these into an order of how likely you would be to believe them, you would probably put (6) and (8) pretty low down. The person with an addiction might be suffering with delusions based on the substances they have been using, so what they claim to have seen might not be reliable. It might also be said that someone with an addiction problem is more likely to need to fund a potentially expensive habit, and therefore might result to deception to get the next hit. (6), the gullible person, is not the sort of person who is wilfully trying to deceive you, but they might themselves be deluded. They are the sort of person who will believe anything they are told without any reflection on whether it is true. This person might be fun to gossip with, but they are not a reliable source of information.

(1), (2), (3) and (4) would probably be people you would normally rely on. Your parents brought you up, and for most people, most of the time, parents try to do things to help their children. In most cases, they do not try to delude them. Close friends and siblings also come into this category: generally, we can and do rely on those closest to us to tell us the truth.

Turning to (4), people believe what teachers say, because their job is to be a trustworthy source of knowledge on a certain subject. Telling you things reliably and accurately, and getting you to understand and apply that knowledge well is what teachers do, so it is not surprising that they are considered trustworthy. Note though, that only tells us that teachers are trustworthy in a certain field, not that they will give a generally reliable account of anything. With certain people, perhaps, we can demonstrate that they are reliable in certain areas and not in others.

The case of (5), the expert, is similar. We would perhaps consider them reliable in their field, but perhaps we should not assume that they are generally reliable. If someone collapsed on a train, you might call for a doctor, and trust them to know what to do. You are unlikely to trust them in the case of a fault with the mechanics of the train.

Interestingly, people such as lawyers, doctors, teachers, religious leaders and academics, amongst others, are often taken to be generally reliable people. This is recognised in the handling of certain legal documents; these people are often called upon to do things such as confirm identity for passports and driving licences, for example.

Expertise in a certain field does seem to persuade people that someone is reliable more generally speaking. A famous psychological experiment called the **MILGRAM EXPERIMENT** demonstrates exactly this point. The experiment was set up to make volunteers think they were administering stronger and stronger electric shocks to other volunteers, as punishment for getting answer wrong to certain questions. Volunteers were told that it was a psychological study of learning; it was actually about how the volunteers responded to authority. It was found that in the vast majority of cases, volunteers could be made to give what they believed were fatal electric shocks to people in another room on the instruction of someone in authority, namely the person running the experiment. This not only shows how easily people divest themselves of moral responsibility (an interesting question, but not relevant here), but also how easily people's behaviour changes in response to those in authority.

In the case of (7), we cannot know whether or not they are reliable. We have nothing to go on at all. However, we do rely on what total strangers tell us quite often. We ask strangers for directions; we believe them when they tell us that this bus is always late, or that train was cancelled last week. Unless we have a reason for thinking a stranger is unreliable, we generally treat things told to us by strangers as credible. Of course, this will all come down to what the stranger is telling us.

What Are They Claiming?

We cannot just consider who is telling us something; we must also consider what they are telling us. There are some things that we would find hard to believe, even if our most trusted friend told us. There are other things that we would be happy to believe, whoever told us.

Perhaps the more unlikely the event, the fewer people we believe? It makes sense to say that we would believe a total stranger if they were telling us something that we already found plausible, such as the fact that this bus is always late, but that we would not believe them if they told us something implausible, such as the fact that the city was abolishing all bus routes.

Conversely, there are some events that might be so extraordinary that it would not matter how reliable the person was; you would still find it incredible. If your mother, brother or best friend told you that they had seen someone being raised from the dead, you would probably find it hard to believe them, and you would in all likelihood be looking for more evidence, at least, before agreeing that it happened.

So, when something is very likely, or very unimportant, we might believe anyone, or at least many people; conversely, when something is very unlikely, or very important, even the testimony of our most trusted friends might not be sufficient.

Miraculous claims are so extraordinary, they are inherently difficult to believe. Moreover, biblical accounts of miracles rely on eye-witness reports that are over two thousand years old.

Witnesses

Eye-witness testimony is often used in criminal prosecutions to establish the facts of the case, or to establish the identity of the person who committed the crime. Juries are swayed by eye-witness testimony, yet lots of psychological research suggests that witnesses are far less reliable than we might think.

It is tempting to think that the key to finding out what happened in a crime, or who perpetrated it, is to find someone who was there, who can testify to the details of the case. It might be thought that an eye-witness is the next-best thing to CCTV footage: perhaps the jury cannot see what happened, but the witness did. But human memory is not like a video recorder. CCTV records everything that is there; the human mind searches for relevance, and is always trying to understand new experiences in the light of past experiences. Our minds do not simply record events; they interpret them as they happen, so the witness account is only the event as they recollect it.

Moreover, memory is a notoriously slippery thing. In a stressful situation, the mind focuses on the important things: specifics about what the perpetrator was wearing, for example, might not be remembered; the order of events, as the person remembers them, might be incorrect. It has been shown that in many cases where a conviction was overturned, incorrect eye-witness testimony had formed part of the evidence in the original trial.

Furthermore, the work of psychologists such as **ELIZABETH LOFTUS** has shown that false memories can actually be created. Loftus established that memory is a very malleable thing, and can easily fall foul of misinformation. That is to say that you can actually change a witness's memory, or alter its focus, by introducing misinformation. Even if the witness believes themselves to be giving a wholly accurate account of what happened, it does not seem to follow that their testimony is reliable.

This must have implications for the study of miracles. If a witness cannot give an accurate testimony of a crime, then it follows that eye-witness testimony from two thousand years ago is unlikely to be reliable. We will look more at this kind of thinking when we consider Hume's critique of miracles later on.

Multiple witnesses

Perhaps one witness can be unreliable, but maybe many witnesses to the same event would convince us that it happened. If on 9/11, there was only one person saying it had happened, it might perhaps have been thought to be a tasteless hoax, or that the person was deceived in some way. But the fact that everyone was talking about it, and it was on every television channel, made it practically incontrovertible that it had taken place.

Many biblical miracles claim to have lots of eye-witnesses; most notably, of course, in the case of the feeding of the five thousand. If there were five thousand people there, then it seems that the account of what happened is bound to be more reliable.

But five thousand witnesses might not afford the reassurance that they seem to. For a start, just because it is reported as an event where five thousand people were fed, that does not count as five thousand eye-witnesses. After all, we do not have five thousand accounts from those who claimed to see the event. Moreover, the sources for our knowledge of this event, the Four Gospels, were written years after the event, not at the time.

Furthermore, even if we did have five thousand accounts, each claiming that Jesus fed them and four thousand nine hundred and ninety-nine others, even that might not make the accounts plausible. There is a psychological phenomenon called **GROUPTHINK**. Groupthink is a kind of conformity of thinking that occurs when a group of people no longer think as individuals, but as part of a group, and come to different and sometimes illogical conclusions as a result.

An example of groupthink comes through this established experiment. A group of actors pretending to be volunteers, plus one real volunteer, are brought in to answer certain questions. The volunteer is told that the questions are about perception. Each member of the group is asked a very simple question, such as "Which line is longer?", where it is completely obvious which is longer. All the fake volunteers answer incorrectly. Usually, when the real volunteer is asked, they will then give the same wrong answer as the rest of the group. Pack mentality, or the desire to conform, or loyalty to the group, has overridden logic and reason.

In the case of miracles, therefore, the existence of more witnesses does not necessarily make the event more plausible.

WHAT MAKES OUR OWN SENSORY EXPERIENCES CREDIBLE?

We might have seen many reasons not to trust witness reports, but we might be more inclined to believe what we see with our own eyes.

Consider the following:

- You see someone walk past your window.

- You see someone you know in the distance.

- You see a ghost floating past your house.

- You see an ill person recover completely.

- You speak to a relative on the phone.

- You see someone halt a tornado.

We use sense data all the time to establish what is true. We look around us to see what is there, and form beliefs about what the world is like based on what we perceive. But seeing is not always believing, and in certain cases, we might distrust what we think we saw.

You would be credulous about (1) very easily. After all, it frequently happens that people walk past windows. If you were to think carefully about the other options, (perhaps it could have been a hologram designed to deceive you, or you could have been dreaming or hallucinating) the mundane nature of the event would probably persuade you that it is more likely that things are exactly as they seem.

You might be slightly less credulous about (2) and (5). Many of us will have experienced that embarrassing moment of waving at someone we know, and then realising that they are actually someone who looks very

much like someone we know. In the case of speaking to a relative on the phone, we are usually pretty convinced that it is them speaking, but you can imagine a case where one cousin sounds like another cousin, so you think you are speaking to one, not the other.

You might or might not be credulous about (4). After all, we see people recover completely from illnesses all the time: we regularly see people get better after having had a cold or flu. What would you think, though, if someone had a serious disease that went away as soon as someone placed his hands on them? What if you saw someone who you knew could not walk get up and take steps across the room? We have already said that in more extraordinary events, we might not even take the accounts of those closest to us to be reliable, but would we believe our own senses? If our eyes are a reliable method for discovering that someone has walked past our window, why stop relying on them when it comes to something more extraordinary? If our senses are generally reliable, does it not make more sense to believe what they tell us?

If you ever find yourself doubting your senses, you surely will doubt them in the case of (3) and (6). As far as extraordinary events go, these are wholly in that category. They would require, in the case of (3), the existence of ghosts, and in the case of (6), for someone to have complete control over nature. Because these events are so extraordinary, perhaps you might look for other explanations for what you saw. You might do a bit of research into other explanations for sightings of ghosts, such as certain hormonal behaviour or the presence of certain electromagnetic waves. You might say to yourself that the halting of the tornado was coincidence - the man held up his hand, and the tornado stopped, but those two things could be **CORRELATED AND NOT CAUSALLY RELATED** - they happened one after the other, but it might not necessarily follow that the man holding up his hand caused the tornado to stop.

Can we believe what we see?

DESCARTES, in The Meditations, suggested that if our senses ever deceive us, we should perhaps not rely on them at all. Many of us have had dreams that seemed real, or have seen things out of the corner of our eye that turned out not to be accurate. What we perceive and what is the case are not always the same thing. If our senses are sometimes unreliable, then why assume that they are ever reliable? If you have had dreams that seemed real there is a possibility that you are dreaming right now. We said earlier that we would be more likely to believe that a person had walked past your window than a ghost, but why think this? We would say it is more likely, based on what is usual to perceive, but we have already shown that our senses are not always a reliable method of finding out what is true.

Descartes even questions whether we can know that the external world is there at all: if we cannot trust what we perceive, then why not entertain the idea that our mind is the only thing that exists, and our perception of our body and the world around us is a deception created by the manipulations of an evil demon? If our senses cannot be relied upon, we can give no evidence that this is not the case.

QUINE, an American 20th-C philosopher, would entirely disagree with Descartes' analysis of belief. Descartes questions all beliefs on the basis that some of them are problematic, but Quine posits the idea of a **WEB OF BELIEF**. We should not throw out all our beliefs if one of them is shown to be unreliable; rather we should only throw out beliefs that do not cohere with our beliefs in general. The web of beliefs is a construction of all our beliefs, which must all fit together. For example, we cannot believe that it is both Tuesday and Sunday. How do we know which belief to throw out? Well, our belief that yesterday was Monday would cohere better with our belief that today is Tuesday, so the belief that it is Sunday has to go.

Quine claimed that there were some beliefs that we would easily revise or reject, and some beliefs that we would only consider throwing out under extreme circumstances. I would happily give up the belief that someone in London is wearing purple socks today - it is hardly central to my thinking - but I would not give up the belief that 2+2=4 anywhere near as easily. In the case of miraculous events, they call into question some of your most central beliefs, such as the laws of logic and physics, and so it would be harder to incorporate a belief in the miraculous event into your thinking, as it would require the rejection of beliefs that lie at the heart of your world view.

RICHARD SWINBURNE - THE PRINCIPLES OF CREDULITY AND TESTIMONY

RICHARD SWINBURNE argues that we can believe both what we see, and the testimony of others, much more than we think we can. He argues on the basis of probability that our own perceptions, as well as the perceptions of others, are reliable, even in the case of extraordinary events. It is worth noting here that the Principles of Credulity and Testimony are relevant to discussions both of miracles and equally to discussions of religious experience.

The Principle of Credulity

In The Existence of God, Swinburne describes the Principle of Credulity as follows:

> ... if it seems ... to a subject that x is present (and has some characteristic), then probably x is present (and has that characteristic); what one seems to perceive is probably so. - Swinburne, R. Existence of God, p. 303

We make use of this principle all the time in our everyday lives. If I perceive that it is hot in this room, then it is probably the case that it is indeed hot in this room. There are circumstances in which that would not be right, such as if I had a fever, or was wearing all my jumpers at once, but in normal circumstances, if I perceive x, then x is probably true.

Swinburne would apply this principle more widely than everyday experiences; he believes that the principle can be generally applied to all experiences. So, if we go back to our example of my seeing a man halt a tornado, we could say that if I perceive that a man holds up his hand and the tornado halts, then that event probably occurred, so long as I am not dreaming or hallucinating. Similarly, if I see a man who could not walk get up and takes steps across the room, I can say that, all things being equal, this happened.

The Principle of Testimony

Later on in The Existence of God, Swinburne adds to the Principle of Credulity, giving a further principle, one about testimony. He describes the Principle of Testimony as follows:

> ... (in the absence of special considerations) the experiences of others are (probably) as they report them. - Swinburne, Existence of God, p. 322

So, as long as there are no special reasons to think otherwise, we can trust others to report things correctly; the testimony of others is generally reliable. Mitigating circumstances might be, for example:

- that someone is hallucinating, either because of some kind of psychotic disorder, or because of drug use.

- that someone has a good reason to lie about what they saw, especially when it will directly benefit them.

- that someone has not got the intellectual capacity or experience to interpret the event correctly, for example if someone from an isolated tribe reported that people climbed into a bird and flew, having seen an aeroplane.

- that someone has been persuaded that something is true when it is not, such as in the example of groupthink above.

If no mitigating factor can be found, then the testimony of others can be held to be reliable.

Again, this is a principle we make use of every day. If we see someone shouting at a person whom we cannot see, and that person tells us that the invisible person is trying to kill them, we will assume that they are suffering with a kind of psychotic disorder. On the other hand, if someone ran towards you with terror in their eyes, and said someone was chasing them with a knife, you would probably believe them, however unusual that kind of event is.

As with the Principle of Credulity, Swinburne does not just apply the Principle of Testimony to everyday occurrences. We can believe people's accounts about more extraordinary events, provided there are no mitigating reasons for us not to.

All things being equal, Swinburne argues, we can trust what we see and what others say irrespective of whether the event is everyday or not. Of course, when it comes to an incredible event like a report of a miracle, there may be more reasons to doubt the testimony. However, if there are no mitigating circumstances, Swinburne claims that we should admit that it probably happened.

Evaluation

By recognising that we employ the Principles of Credulity and Testimony all the time in everyday life, and accounting for circumstances in which it is not reasonable to believe what we see and what we hear from others, Swinburne has cleverly shifted the burden of proof onto the sceptic. This means the sceptic now has the responsibility to show why miracles could not happen, rather than asking advocates to argue for why they could.

By employing these principles and accounting for circumstances when we would not use them, he has allowed for a miraculous event to be analysed in exactly the same way as any other event.

Imagine you saw someone raised from the dead. You would certainly ask yourself the questions: "am I dreaming?"; "did someone slip me a hallucinogen?"; "was he really dead?". When you were convinced, however, that everything was as it seemed to be, what other conclusion could you come to, other than that the man had been resurrected? Swinburne's Principles of Credulity and Testimony allow for us to use everyday common sense, applying it whenever there is no reason not to.

However, it could be argued that the principles are only applicable to everyday occurrences. The principles are claiming that if something seems a certain way, or someone says something has happened, then everything being equal, it probably is that way. But the key here is the word "probably".

Let's look at two examples to draw out the problem:

EXAMPLE 1 - My sister says she has seen a duck. There are no reasons to disbelieve her, so I conclude that she probably has.

EXAMPLE 2 - My sister says she has seen someone raised from the dead. There are no reasons to disbelieve her, so I conclude that she probably has.

In example 1, my conclusion that my sister probably has seen a duck is not based purely on whether she is a reliable witness; it is also based on whether having seen a duck is a likely occurrence at all. As my sister lives right by a river, it is extremely likely that she would see a duck. Even if she did not live by a river, I know that ducks exist, and that people see them. It is fair, in this case, to conclude that my sister has, indeed, seen a duck.

Example 2 might seem similar, and you might argue that if my sister is a reliable witness to the duck, she is a reliable witness to the resurrection. But seeing a duck is an event that I know is in the gamut of possible events; I know what it means to say that she probably saw a duck. How could I possibly ascribe probability to an event so wholly removed from my experience as a resurrection would be? **HUME** would argue that there is so much evidence from experience that this never happens that we can know it to be improbable that it did. Even if I know that my sister is neither a liar nor was she under the influence of a hallucinogen, it is still more likely that she was mistaken in some way, however difficult that might be to explain. Hume argues that we should always believe the **LESSER MIRACLE**; in this case, that my sister was mistaken, rather than the greater miracle, that she truly did see someone rise from the dead.

Even if you were willing to admit that if someone says they have witnessed a resurrection then they probably have, all things being equal, it still does not really get you anywhere. What Swinburne has effectively done is come up with principles that say "if you think you see x, and you are reliable, your perception that you saw x is reliable" and "if Bert said he saw x, and he is reliable, then his report that he saw x is reliable". This is effectively **TAUTOLOGICAL**; it is not really telling us anything. The whole question at stake is whether a miraculous event is or could ever be witnessed reliably, or is it, as Hume argues, always more likely that the miracle has not occurred? Swinburne is not really answering this question.

Furthermore, psychological research does seem to bear out the fact that eye-witness testimony, even from groups of people, is extremely unreliable. Swinburne is trading on the fact that it is "probably" as they report it, but given that experiments show that testimonies are less reliable than we would like to think, and that juries give undue weight to them, does Swinburne have the right to say that anything is "probably" as it is reported to us?

CONCLUSION

For everyday events, we are happy to deal in "probably" when it comes to believing what we see, and what others tell us. If we treated all events with the kind of scepticism that Descartes employs, we would live a life paralysed by doubt about what we can and cannot be sure of. Miracles are, however, not normal events - that is what makes them miraculous - so the "probably" we are happy to apply to normal occurrences might not be enough here.

KEY TERMS

- **CREDIBLE** - How believable something is.

- **CREDULOUS** - How believing a person is, e.g. I will be credulous, if you are saying something credible.

- **GROUPTHINK** - The psychological phenomenon where people report, and are even persuaded by, different things if they are part of a group.

- **WEB OF BELIEF** - Quine's view that our beliefs are an interconnected web, where we reject things based on the fact that they do not cohere with the rest of the web. Some things, such as the truths of Maths and Logic, are more central to this web, and hence less easily given up, than other things.

- **PRINCIPLES OF CREDULITY AND TESTIMONY** - Swinburne's principles that support the idea that we can generally believe what we see and what is reported to us by others.

SELF-ASSESSMENT QUESTIONS

1. If you had to formulate three criteria for credibility, what would they be?

2. If you saw a ghost, would you be more likely to believe in ghosts or that you were mistaken?

3. If there is no reason to distrust a witness, would all events he reported seeing be plausible?

FURTHER READING

- **DESCARTES, R** - Meditations, translated DM Clarke, Penguin , 2010, especially the First Meditation

- **LEWIS, CS** - Miracles, Collins, 1947

- **SWINBURNE, R** - The Existence of God, 3rd ed. OUP, 2004, Ch .12

Miracles & the Attributes of God

The idea of a God that acts in the world to cause miracles is one that scholars such as Nelson Pyke and Stewart Sutherland find inconsistent with the attributes that God is said to have. God is said to be wholly simple, immutable (incapable of change) and eternal. These attributes seem to be in tension with the idea of a God that acts.

DIVINE SIMPLICITY AND IMMUTABILITY

God is held to be wholly simple. This means that He is not composed of parts; He is indivisible. Related to this is the idea that God is immutable; unchanging. As Sutherland notes, if God is simple and immutable, then the idea of His acting is decidedly questionable: how can He act if He cannot change?

Think about the example of getting up and having breakfast. You go from being asleep to being awake. You move from your bed to the bedroom door, put on your dressing gown and head downstairs. You switch on the coffee machine and put a bagel in the toaster. Once everything is ready, you sit down and eat your breakfast whilst listening to the Today programme on Radio 4.

These are everyday human actions, but they require the ability to change. Even in these ten minutes the following changes have taken place:

1.   You have gone from being asleep to being awake

2.   You have gone from lying down to standing up

3.   You have gone from being in your pyjamas to also wearing a dressing gown

4.   You have gone from being upstairs to being downstairs

5.   You have moved your hand and switched the coffee machine on

6.   You have moved your hand and toasted a bagel

7.   You have ingested breakfast and started to metabolise it

8. You have gained knowledge you did not previously have through listening to the radio

Actions mean change. We are not immutable beings; quite the contrary, we are always changing. We are able to act because we are able to change. On the **ARISTOTELIAN** view, change happens when something moves from being potentially x to being actually x. According to Aristotle, God would have to be pure act with no potential. This is why Aristotle's Prime Mover is both unaware of the world as well as uninvolved with the world. The Prime Mover could never cause miracles.

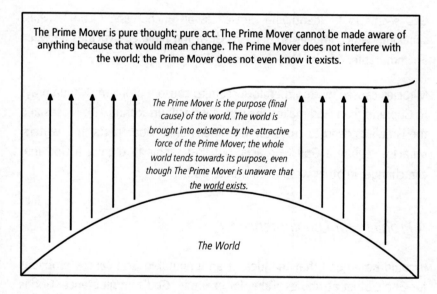

The Prime Mover is pure thought; pure act. The Prime Mover cannot be made aware of anything because that would mean change. The Prime Mover does not interfere with the world; the Prime Mover does not even know it exists.

The Prime Mover is the purpose (final cause) of the world. The world is brought into existence by the attractive force of the Prime Mover; the whole world tends towards its purpose, even though The Prime Mover is unaware that the world exists.

The World

The Christian tradition was influenced by the Aristotelian tradition, largely through St Thomas Aquinas and other **SCHOLASTIC THINKERS**. It could be argued that the Christian understanding of, on the one hand, immutability has been influenced by Aristotle's view, but that the idea of God's acting in the world, on the other hand, is also well established through what is said in the Bible. Perhaps Christianity is labouring under mixed messages.

Moreover, in places, the Bible seems to suggest that God is both immutable and a being that acts, sometimes even at the same time. Take this example from Exodus 3, where God speaks to Moses in a burning bush:

> God said to Moses, "I am who I am. This is what you are to say to the Israelites: 'I am has sent me to you.'" (Exodus 3:14)

God seems to be identifying Himself as an unchanging "I am", whilst speaking, which implies an act. Arguably, the Bible equivocates between an immutable, unchanging God, and a God who acts.

Miracles caused by God therefore seem to cause a problem. Joshua prays to God and then God makes the sun stand still (in Joshua 10); Moses and the Israelites need to cross the Red Sea and God parts the waters. Miracles require a God who acts, but that seems to require a God that can change; in other words, a mutable God.

A Problem for Omnipotence?

It could be argued that the idea of an immutable God causes problems for God's other attributes. Take, for example, God's omnipotence. God is said to be all-powerful, which is to say that He can do anything, but if He is immutable then perhaps this limits what He can do. Not only would it make Him incapable of change, but it would seem to make Him incapable of any kind of action; quite a limit to omnipotence.

It could be argued, as Aquinas does, that God's omnipotence entails only the things that can be done, and only the things that are **CONSISTENT WITH GOD'S NATURE**. So God does not need to be able to do things which cannot be done, such as making a square circle, and He does not need to be able to do things that contradict His nature, such as acting, despite the fact that He is immutable.

Still, it seems that if we mean by immutable "unable to change", and hence "unable to act", then God's omnipotence seems to have been gravely limited. What kind of omnipotence could God have if He cannot act? It sounds not like omnipotence, but rather impotence.

Divine Eternity

This problem is further compounded by the fact that God is said to be eternal; that is to say, that He is said to be outside of time. Yet miracles take place at specific moments; they happen in time. How could a being that is timeless act in time? Miracles are brief, transient occurrences; they do not happen eternally.

One could suggest an understanding of eternity as "everlasting" rather than "timeless". This would allow God to exist in time, but to have a life that is infinite rather than finite.

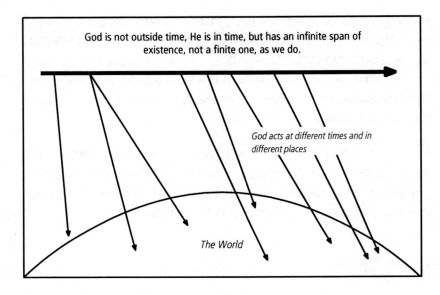

God is not outside time, He is in time, but has an infinite span of existence, not a finite one, as we do.

God acts at different times and in different places

The World

But this seems unhelpful because then it seems that God is subject to time; He cannot have created time if He exists in time. This seems not to be consistent with the idea of God as omnipotent as well as the idea of God as creator of the world ex nihilo, out of nothing. Moreover, it calls into question God's immutability, as He seems to do different things at different times; He would therefore also cease to be changeless on this model.

A Solution to All of These Problems?

St Thomas Aquinas offers a solution that might go some way to alleviating all of these apparent problems in the attributes of God. He suggests that an immutable and eternal God could perform one single, timeless action, the effect of which is perceived as actions taking place at a specific place and time. This would be consistent with the idea that

God is immutable, and uses the Aristotelian idea that God is pure act, as God would not have to go from being potentially x to being actually x.

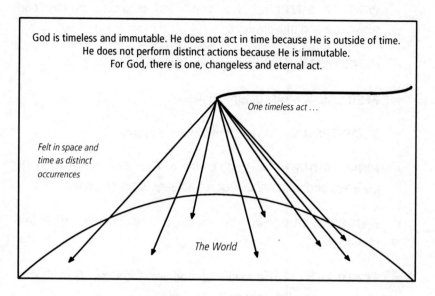

God is timeless and immutable. He does not act in time because He is outside of time. He does not perform distinct actions because He is immutable. For God, there is one, changeless and eternal act.

One timeless act . . .

Felt in space and time as distinct occurrences

The World

A good example to explain Aquinas's point of view might be the idea of the sun. The sun shines all time: it shines in the night-time; it shines when it is behind a cloud. From what we perceive, the sun starts shining every morning, and sets at night; it stops shining when a cloud moves in front of it. What seems to us a sun that appears and disappears, shining in specific times and places, is not really so.

Similarly, our perception of miracles might be that they are specific events, resulting from a specific action that took place at a certain time, but our perception might be wrong. Just as the sun shines always, it could be that God changelessly and eternally acts.

KEY TERMS

- **WHOLLY SIMPLE** - Not composed of parts; wholly one substance and indivisible.

- **IMMUTABLE** - Unchanging and unchangeable.

- **ETERNAL** - Outside of time; timeless.

- **SEMPITERNAL** - In time, but always existing.

- **PRIME MOVER** - Aristotle's idea of God. The Prime Mover is pure act, and immutable, but is unaware of his creation.

- **ARISTOTELIAN** - In the tradition surrounding Aristotle's philosophy.

- **SCHOLASTIC** - The medieval tradition from the 13th C that centres around the writings of Aristotle.

SELF-ASSESSMENT QUESTIONS

1. Could God be immutable and still act?

2. Could an eternal God act in time?

3. Does Aquinas's solution to questions of God's attributes provide a good answer, or complicate things further?

FURTHER READING

- **AQUINAS** - Summa Theologiae, First Part, Question 9, Article 1

- **DAVIES, B** - An Introduction to the Philosophy of Religion, 3rd ed. OUP, 2004, pp. 257-259

- **VARDY, P & ARLISS, J** - The Thinker's Guide to God, John Hunt Publishing, 2003, pp. 150-154

A Critique of Miracles - David Hume

In the first Chapter, we discussed Hume's approach to the topic of miracles, examining the definition he gives, and reasons why he may have defined miracles in that way.

We have already noted that:

1. Hume was an empiricist, and believed that sense data are the ultimate basis of all knowledge.

2. Hume is well known for his apparent scepticism about arguments for the existence of God in Dialogues Concerning Natural Religion.

3. Hume defined miracles as "a transgression of a Law of Nature by the particular volition of the Deity, or by the interposition of one of His invisible agents".

4. Hume's definition is extremely prescriptive, and allows for fewer kinds of events to be described as miraculous than other definitions.

5. Hume's definition of miracles is given in a different context to most definitions. The other definitions of the term miracle we have looked at have been from those who believe miracles can occur; this definition is given in the context of a critique

6. The highly precise nature of Hume's definition plays to the arguments he gives in his critique. His definition is such that he can argue that such events do not happen.

Hume's Critique

In **AN ENQUIRY CONCERNING HUMAN UNDERSTANDING** Hume approaches his critique of miracles from two directions. Firstly, he gives what **CLACK AND CLACK** describe as an **A PRIORI ARGUMENT** for the non-occurrence of miracles; an argument that argues that miracles could never happen. Secondly, he gives what we might call an **AD HOMINEM** attack on testimonies about miracles; one that focuses on the reliability of the accounts of miracles.

The A Priori Argument

Hume is part of a great British tradition of **EMPIRICISM**. Like John Locke before him, and AJ Ayer after him, Hume believed that evidence, and specifically sense data, were very important in drawing conclusions about the way the world is. This might seem commonsensical to us now - "seeing is believing" could be the motto for our modern world view - but it was not always like this. The modern world view, with its emphasis on evidence from the senses, is only one possible way of understanding the world, and it was a view that developed thanks to the work of people like Locke and Hume.

THE WISE MAN, says Hume, **APPORTIONS HIS BELIEF TO THE EVIDENCE**. That is to say that the wise man believes only the things which evidence supports. Now, when we look at the evidence around us, we are struck by a world in which we never see laws of nature broken; our experience is uniformly that the laws of nature apply unfailingly at all times and in all places. So, when presented with a testimony that a miracle has taken place, the weight of evidence against this event is huge. Up against all the trillions of times the laws of nature have held, this one event provides minimal evidence that the law has been broken.

Hume argues that it is always more likely that the law of nature had held rather than having been broken. We have "a uniform experience against every miraculous event": all our experience is of nature holding, and this outweighs greatly any possibility that a law of nature has broken.

As Clack and Clack put it, what Hume has effectively done is formulated an argument that runs like this:

> A miracle is "a violation of a law of nature"
> A law of nature cannot be violated
> Therefore, no miracle can occur.
>
> Clack and Clack, The Philosophy of Religion, p. 146

The Argument Against Testimony

Hume's next argument is one we might call an **AD HOMINEM** argument. Ad hominem arguments, literally arguments "to the man", are ones that argue based on the characteristics of a person. So, for example, I might give an ad hominem argument against listening to x's argument if he or she has limited knowledge of that field, or is an inveterate liar. Ad hominem arguments are not focused on your opponent's view; they are focused on your opponent himself.

Hume's ad hominem argument focuses on the people who testify to the occurrence of miracles. We have already seen that Hume believes that "the wise man apportions his belief to the evidence", and the evidence is weighed against the occurrence of miracles. Hume therefore suspects that those who are able to ignore what he sees to be overwhelming evidence against miracles might not be wise. His argument put simply is that no testimony is trustworthy enough to overcome the uniform evidence of laws of nature holding.

Hume makes his case by focusing on four main points:

▶ There are never sufficient testimonies from educated and reliable witnesses

When we think about the accounts of miracles we have from, for example, the Bible, the vast majority of the events were purportedly witnessed by people who were illiterate, and were in no way authoritative figures. Hume evidently thinks there is a correlation between someone's educational level and his or her propensity to believe in miracles.

▶ People are easily dazzled, and prone to believe in exciting and wondrous things

Hume claimed that people want to believe in exciting things, and easily suspend reason in order to believe that something extraordinary has occurred. He claims that people, especially if they have a reason to do so (such as the fact that it would support their religious belief), will happily believe something wondrous has occurred, even if the evidence against it is substantial. In this way he anticipates some of the conclusions of modern psychological research, which has demonstrated that what people believe they see and hear can be shaped by their prior beliefs and expectations (see Chapter 7). Even when trying in good faith to be completely honest, we have a surprising ability to deceive ourselves.

▸ The miraculous events occur in "ignorant and barbarous nations"

In what must be one of the most memorable phrases in Western Philosophy, Hume is now directly attacking not just the specific people who testify that miracles have happened, but the times and places in which they lived. This point might be shocking to our politically correct sensitivities, but perhaps this is what Hume meant: 1st-C Palestine, where biblical reports of miracles took place, was somewhere in which the vast majority of people were illiterate and poor. Illness and disability were understood as being due to the sins of the person's father or mother. Having certain diseases would see you ostracised completely from society. Women could be stoned to death for sleeping with a married man. Put this way, we can see what Hume meant: that testimonies about miracles are frequent in places where people's education and opportunities are low. From his place at the centre of the Scottish Enlightenment he would have heard very few if any accounts of miracles.

▸ Miracles are "contrary facts"; they occur in all faiths and can therefore not be used to verify one religion over another

Here, Hume moves away slightly from a direct attack on those who testify that miracles have occurred to make a quite subtle and clever argument. As we saw earlier, many religions have stories of the miraculous at the centre of their faith. Now, if each faith claims that these miracles verify the truth of their religion, we come to a problem, if one assumes that these faiths are in conflict, and not all of them can be true. If all religions claim that miracles verify their religion over others, then in practice no miracle can verify that a faith position is true; they cancel each other out.

Is Hume Right About Miracles?

There are a number of reasons to suggest that Hume has made astute arguments against the occurrence of miracles. As we already said, Hume anticipated modern psychology in recognising that people want to believe exciting and fantastical things. Moreover, psychological studies have confirmed a lot of what Hume said about how unreliable testimony is.

Hume's argument about the weight of evidence that is against miracles also seems plausible. We live in a world that seems to operate according to certain laws that uniformly apply at all times and in all places. Everything we have ever experienced counts against the occurrence of miracles, from this point of view.

However, there are a number of areas where Hume's critique seems lacking.

Laws of Nature

The idea that we live in a universe governed by certain unbreakable laws of nature is one that is incompatible with the idea that scientific conclusions are only provisional; further evidence can always falsify them. The universe is not governed by laws; the laws of nature are humanity's way of describing what it has discovered so far. What we have is our best hypothesis based on current evidence, but sometimes there will be new phenomena that need to be accounted for. On this view, something that to Hume would seem like a "transgression of a law of nature" would be new evidence to apply to the established ideas of the way the world is. Something that is not in line with previous scientific conclusions does not break the law; it exposes the law as having never been correct in the first place.

Seen this way Hume's argument that it is always more likely that the law of nature has held simply does not hold up. Scientists are used to finding new evidence that calls into question prior conclusions. Indeed, scientific progress would be impossible if scientists were not open to the possibility that conclusions might need to be revised or refined.

Hume was, understandably for his time, working on a Newtonian model of science as a system governed by universal laws that prescribe which events are physically possible, and which are impossible. Swinburne pointed out that laws of nature do not prescribe what can happen; they only describe what we know so far to have happened.

Nevertheless, if the overwhelming majority our experience says that people do not spontaneously levitate or rise from the dead, then it would and should take a lot to convince scientists that our previous scientific conclusions need rethinking. The fact that the weight of evidence is against this event should arguably make anyone sceptical about its veracity. Swinburne's correction of Hume's understanding of the laws of nature does not undermine the huge weight of evidence we have that these kinds of event do not occur. What has been successfully refuted, however, is the idea that a law of nature is never revisable on the basis of new evidence.

Probability

Moreover, Hume seems to be making claims of probability based solely on what he has already experienced. This is not surprising given that Hume is an empiricist, but as **CS LEWIS** notes, if you base your world view on the world as experienced, no account of miracles will ever persuade you; you will conclude that it is improbable. Keith Ward argues that probability cannot be determined on its own - something is not inherently probable - something is probable within a certain context. In the context of a world view that contains God, miracles might not seem that improbable, whereas in a world view that is comprised only of beliefs based on things sensed, miracles seem less probable.

Furthermore, it is worth noting that by their very nature, miracles are bound to be improbable. If miracles were natural, everyday occurrences, we would never notice them, for a start, and they would hardly be best described as miraculous! A critique of miracles that is based on how unlike the normal state of thing they are risks missing the very thing that a miracle is.

Ad Hominem Arguments

Moving on from Hume's first argument, now let us evaluate his arguments against those who testify the fact miracles have taken place. We called Hume's argument about testimony an ad hominem argument because it attacks the type of person who claims to witness a miracle, and not the likelihood of a miracle occurring. Hume points out that, amongst witnesses who testify about miracles: they are not intelligent or educated enough; they are likely to want to believe exciting things; they will be easily persuaded of a miracle if they already have strong religious faith; they tend to come from "ignorant and barbarous nations".

Ad hominem arguments are widely deemed to be fallacious ways of arguing. Rather than addressing what someone is saying, you attack them instead. Take these two statements:

1. David Cameron's policies do not sufficiently address poverty because he went to Eton.

2. David Cameron's policies do not sufficiently address poverty because in a global recession, his priorities lie elsewhere.

The first statement is an ad hominem attack; one that we frequently see being made in the press. The fact that David Cameron went to Eton is being used here to imply that he is therefore clueless about poverty. Never mind that he studied Philosophy, Politics and Economics at university, or the fact that Eton offers bursaries to students who cannot afford the fees; it is assumed that because he went to Eton, he is not interested in helping the poor.

We can see that the second statement gives a reason why poverty might not be adequately addressed - it is not the highest priority for government. That would not at all absolve him of blame - we might argue that he has got his priorities wrong - but it does not assume that he is uninterested in the poor because of his privileged educational background.

Ad hominem attacks are understandable fallacies. They pick on a person's traits and use them to undermine his or her argument. We might think a person's characteristics make his or her argument less plausible, but actually they are independent. The reason that they are independent is that you can admit that a person has that tendency and still defend that argument. Let's use Hume's examples to show why this is the case.

Witnesses are:

▸ Unintelligent and uneducated; there are never enough educated witnesses

Even if that were true, that would not render their testimony false. Very little education is required to be able to say what you see; you do not need to be a doctor to see someone dead come back to life, or a meteorologist to see a storm stop. There are many things that uneducated people cannot do, but saying what they see ought to be possible, even with a low level of education.

▸ Prone to believe exciting and wondrous events have occurred

People are gullible, and can tend to want to believe something exciting and unlikely over something mundane and more likely. However, that is perfectly compatible with exciting and unlikely events occurring. The fact that someone would like to believe something does not mean that that thing cannot occur.

▸ From "ignorant and barbarous nations"

Arguably, this is just racism uttered at a time when that was more acceptable. But even if you admit that 1st-C Palestine was quite a different time and place to 18th-C Edinburgh, that does not make all biblical witnesses intrinsically unreliable. For a start, not everyone living in a certain time or place has to be alike; there are more and less reliable people everywhere. Moreover, as we said above, testifying to what you have seen requires no special skills, just saying what you see.

Furthermore, this point might have something to say about 1st-C Palestine, but nowadays Lourdes in France is a major centre for pilgrimages and reports of miracles. Surely, no one would call France ignorant and barbarous … would they?

Ad hominem attacks are seen to be fallacious, because they do not attack the argument itself; they attack the person. This misses the point of doing Philosophy, which is all about formulating logical responses to philosophical questions. Having said this, an ad hominem attack arguably has merit in the discussion of miracles. Although we have shown that none of Hume's attacks on witnesses show definitively that miracles could not happen, nevertheless, they might mean we want to question how reliable the witness is. In the case of biblical accounts of miracles, all we have to go on is testimony, and it is therefore reasonable that Hume asks whether we can trust those testimonies.

Hume's discussion is too narrow

SWINBURNE would argue that Hume's definition of a miracle as a "transgression of a law of nature by the particular volition of the Deity or by the interposition of one of his invisible agents" is too narrow as it does not account for the religious significance of the event. Hume's approach to the topic of miracles is very mechanistic; he is interested in whether events of this sort could happen, and whether we can trust those who say that they do. Hume fails to recognise that these are not only reports of events but narratives within a tradition. We can only get a very partial understanding of miracles if we do not look into what significance they might have in the context of a certain faith. It could be argued that Hume is only interested in discussing his idea of miracles - a break in a law of nature - not miracles as they are really seen in the context of the traditions from which they originate.

CONCLUSION

Hume's critique of miracles is memorable and well expressed, giving sound empirical reasons to be wary both of the idea of miracles itself as well as those on whose testimony to the occurrence of miracles we rely. His discussion is, however, limited to whether breaches of laws of nature occur, and thus is working from a scientific paradigm that is no longer in favour, and fails to account for the religious significance of these events beyond their extraordinary nature.

KEY TERMS

- **A PRIORI ARGUMENT** - An argument that relies on no premises from the world of experience, but proceeds from definitions and unequivocal truths to inferring conclusions.

- **AD HOMINEM ATTACK** - A critique based not on what the opponent is saying, but on things about the opponent. This form of attack is usually seen to be fallacious.

- **EMPIRICISM** - The world view that we can know the world through the data that comes to us through our senses.

- **APPORTION** - To dole out; to portion. To apportion x to y is to dole out x in accordance with y. In the context of what Hume is saying, the wise man's belief is proportionate to what the evidence shows.

- **CONTRARY FACTS** - Facts that contradict or rule each other out.

SELF-ASSESSMENT QUESTIONS

1. Are there any circumstances where the weight of evidence would be in favour of a miracle?

2. Is Hume's ad hominem attack warranted in a discussion of miracles?

3. Is Keith Ward right that miracles could be deemed more probable in different world views?

FURTHER READING

- **CLACK, B & CLACK, BR** - The Philosophy of Religion: A Critical Introduction, 2nd ed. Polity Press, 2008, pp. 143-146

- **COLE, P** - Philosophy of Religion, 2nd ed. Hodder Murray, 2009, pp. 65-68

- **DAVIES, B** - An Introduction to the Philosophy of Religion, 3rd ed. OUP, 2004, pp. 241-257

- **HUME, D** - An Enquiry Concerning Natural Religion, section X "Of Miracles"

- **VARDY, P** - The Puzzle of God, 2nd ed. Fount, 1999, pp. 204-208

- **VARDY, P & ARLISS, J** - The Thinker's Guide to God, John Hunt Publishing, 2003, pp. 154-156

A Critique of Miracles - Maurice Wiles

Our first major critique of the idea of a miracle came from David Hume, who was certainly sceptical about certain aspects of religion, even if we are careful to realise that no sources can confirm that he was definitely an atheist. Our second critique comes from quite a different kind of thinker. Hume seems to be outside religion, looking in; Maurice Wiles, on the other hand, was right at the centre of thinking on Philosophy of Religion. A high-ranking Anglican priest and theologian, Wiles was certainly at the centre of thinking in the Church of England. In 1970 he was made Regius Professor of Divinity at Oxford University, which is the Crown's professorial seat for Theology in Oxford; one of the most prestigious roles to have within the field.

In **GOD'S ACTION IN THE WORLD**, the book in which his 1986 Bampton Lectures were published, Wiles argues that God would not be prevented from performing miracles. If we imagine God as an all-powerful deity, there is nothing inconceivable about Him intervening in nature. It would have to be infrequent, as otherwise the natural order would be undermined, but so long as God intervened infrequently, there would be nothing inconceivable about God performing such miracles. So, unlike Hume, Wiles's critique is not based on an argument that laws of nature could not be broken.

Wiles's critique of miracles focuses rather on what the miraculous says about the nature of God. He argues that although God could perform miracles, He would in fact not perform these kinds of action, because a God that performs miracles **WOULD NOT BE OMNIBENEVOLENT**.

Rather than God dipping into space and time now and again to intervene and perform a miracle, Wiles argued that God's action should be seen as one creative and sustaining action, rather than a series of interventions in the natural order.

If we believe that God does intervene to perform miracles, why is it that He does not perform them in the most desperate of circumstances? Why did Jesus turn water into wine at the wedding in Cana, when God then did nothing to prevent the Holocaust? Why did Jesus feed five thousand people, when someone dies of starvation every three seconds? **THE PROBLEM OF EVIL** will emerge if our model of God is of one who intervenes periodically in nature.

> *... it would seem strange that no miraculous intervention prevented Auschwitz or Hiroshima, while the purposes apparently forwarded by some of the miracles acclaimed in traditional Christian faith seem trivial by comparison. - Maurice Wiles, God's Action in the World, p. 66*

Wiles is happy, rather, to say that it is the symbolic value of miracles which is of value, rather than the actual occurrence of a certain event. As we saw in the chapter on the signs in John's Gospel, there are very good reasons for saying that the miracles are better understood by alluding to their religious significance. However, you might not realise just how unorthodox and controversial this makes Wiles. Christianity has at its heart tales of the miraculous, and to reject that they actually happened means that you reject some of the central tenets of the faith. Wiles came to reject not only more contentious Christian beliefs such as the virgin birth, but also more central ones such as God becoming man in the Incarnation, or Jesus' Resurrection. As his obituary in the Telegraph on 7 June, 2005 said, "he became one of the most radical and controversial scholars of his generation".

Was Wiles Right About Miracles?

Undoubtedly, if God is omnibenevolent, and occasionally intervenes in nature, there are questions to be asked about God's selection. The miracles He seems to choose to perform are not evenly spread in time or place; the profusion of miracles in the time of Jesus and the lack of miracles nowadays might suggest that God is not distributing them fairly. Moreover, as we have already said, it is true that there are cases of God's failure to act that really beg the question of whether He is all good. If God does not intervene in the world, then we can understand why He would fail to prevent massacre or famine, but if He is happy to calm storms and make wine in 1st-C Palestine, and to leave disasters to happen, He seems malevolent indeed.

But perhaps the purpose of miracles is not to minimise suffering. This is the position that **KEITH WARD** has held. Miracles, as we have seen through examining some of the sign narratives in John, often have a **CHRISTOLOGICAL** aim; they are intended to bring people to faith in Christ, or to show something of God's nature. If miracles are supposed to salve wounds and prevent disasters, God would indeed be a favouritist who failed to prevent the suffering of millions of people. But if they are intended to bring people to faith, then it is hardly surprising that there were so many at the time of Jesus. **WARD** agrees with Wiles that if God does act, He must act infrequently, so that the natural order is generally stable, but he sees no reason why miraculous acts would compromise his omnibenevolence.

Wiles preferred to think of God's action as a single act of creation and sustaining that applied not to individual phenomena but to the world as a whole, but as we saw in the chapter on the attributes of God, **AQUINAS** suggested that there is nothing incoherent about God's single, timeless action having effects in particular parts of time and space. The idea of God's action as being indivisible does not rule out the idea of the timeless action of God being felt in time.

Moreover, as **SWINBURNE** notes, if God does not perform miracles, or intervene in the world in any way, what does it mean to say that He is a God in a relationship with his creation? The Christian idea of a responsive God, a God that cares, is wholly undermined. This would also make prayer, or at least intercessionary prayer, where the prayer makes a request, completely pointless, as there would be no hope of an answer. This, it could be argued, is not the God of Theism; it is a deist God, more like Aristotle's Prime Mover; He is a God that has no interaction or relationship with creation.

Wiles further argued that miracle narratives are better understood for their symbolic, rather than for their factual, content. Prima facie, this is extremely plausible, especially given how much symbolism there is in these stories. But yet, just because there is lots of symbolism there, it does not follow that there is nothing else. Just because beneath the initial impression you get of a painting there are brushstrokes, it does not mean that the painting is not there anymore, once you have seen the painting on a deeper level. Perhaps stories of turning water into wine and feeding five thousand people can be understood purely for their symbolic content, but can the same really be said for the Incarnation and the Resurrection?

When Christians are baptised or confirmed, the Creed is said, either on a child's behalf, or by the person themselves when they are old enough. The Creed is the Christian statement of belief. In it we hear the words

> *I believe in Jesus Christ, His [God's] only son, Our Lord*
> *Who was conceived by the Holy Ghost,*
> *Born of the Virgin Mary,*

Suffered under Pontius Pilate,
Was crucified, dead and buried
He descended into Hell.
On the third day, he rose again, according to the scriptures.
He ascended into heaven, and is seated at the right hand of the
Father.

How can Wiles argue that miracles are symbolic, when they are central to the faith of which he himself was a minister? Can Wiles as both a Christian and a priest really claim that God did not in fact become man, and was not raised from the dead?

Moreover, mankind's salvation seems to be linked to God's sacrifice made once and for all on the cross. It is through God's sacrifice that mankind is saved, so if the sacrifice is only symbolic, where does that leave the redemption of mankind?

As Wiles's obituary notes, "to university colleagues, Wiles was a figure of faith; but to his colleagues in the Church he was a figure of doubt, and this he regarded as perfectly proper for a Professor of Divinity".

KEY TERMS

- **OMNIBENEVOLENT** - Literally, "all good wanting"; the property of being wholly good.

- **MALEVOLENT** - The property of wishing evil.

- **INCARNATION**, (The) - When God became man in the person of Jesus Christ.

- **RESURRECTION**, (The) - When Jesus rose from the dead.

- **SALVATION** - The saving of mankind.

- **REDEMPTION** - The healing and forgiveness of mankind.

SELF-ASSESSMENT QUESTIONS

1. Do you think the occurrence of miracles causes problems for God's omnibenevolence?

2. How persuasive is Ward's defence?

3. Can someone be a Christian if they do not believe in the literal truth of the Resurrection?

FURTHER READING

- **VARDY, P** - The Puzzle of God, 2nd ed. Fount, 1999, pp. 208-210

- **VARDY, P & ARLISS, J** - The Thinker's Guide to God, John Hunt Publishing, 2003, pp. 159-161

- **WILES, M** - God's Action in the World: The Bampton Lectures for 1986, SCM Press, 1986

- **WARD, K** - Is Religion Irrational? Lion Books, 2011, Ch. 9

Postscript

Clare Jarmy read Philosophy at St Catharine's College Cambridge, before training to be a teacher. She is Head of Philosophy and Religious Studies at Bedales School in Hampshire.

Students seeking fuller explanations and a bibliography should also consult the website which also contains exam tips and past questions listed by theme.

Lightning Source UK Ltd.
Milton Keynes UK
UKOW04f1844200914

238848UK00001B/19/P